MW01289656

Combat on the Dark Side of the Moon

A true combat story of the Brown Water Navy in Vietnam

by

Charlie Nesbitt

ISBN: 1500847852
ISBN-13: 978-1500847852

Dedication

Combat on the Dark Side of the Moon:

CONTENTS

FORWARD

The dark side of the moon never faces planet Earth. That side of the moon can never be seen with the human eye, it is the mystery part of a planet that we see every night in the starry sky. Combat on the dark side of the moon is a phrase that I think best describes my parent's description of my tour of duty in Vietnam. All they knew was that I was on a part of the planet that was not known to them at the time. It was a place where communication with their son was sketchy at best. They would hope against hope that the knock on the door from a Navy officer bearing bad news would never come. It was just as surreal for them as it was for me to be serving in combat in Vietnam. I found myself on a part of planet Earth that was a mystery to me. It was as if I was cast away to some distant planet where nothing I saw or felt was real. Vietnam did not feel or smell Earth like to me. My tour of duty was an out of this world experience from the very beginning. It was a deployment that I did not know existed in this man's United States Navy.

The mission of the Mobile Riverine Force (MRF), was to transport combat troops of the Army's 9th Infantry Division into and around the hundreds of small water canals of the Mekong Delta, hunting down the Viet Cong in "search and destroy" missions, which turned out to be a very tedious and deadly job. The canals were very narrow, with swift currents and many switchbacks. Tides could surge up or down six to eight feet. The river estuaries and canals were often surrounded by triple canopy jungle, infested with Viet Cong bunkers, which in turn were infested with angry Viet Cong. The hidden enemy had very accurate and deadly B40 and RPG7 rocket propelled grenades. This, as you might expect, is not typical or standard Navy duty, this was Brown Water duty. I truly had no idea what I was getting myself into when my high school friend Doug Morton and I volunteered for this duty while serving in the regular blue water US Navy. (Which I might add was very boring but very safe).

For my entire twelve month duty in Vietnam, I felt like I was on the dark side of the moon for many reasons. First and foremost was this; other than my immediate family, nobody but nobody back in the world gave a shit that I was serving in Vietnam. Also it didn't help that I was involved in the most unpopular foreign war ever in the history of the United States of America.

The word Mobile in the MRF title was just that, we moved around constantly which made mail call a joke. If and when I did receive mail it was postmarked weeks and sometimes months previous (so much for fresh news from home). However the number one reason I felt so out of this world was the lack of discipline aboard the riverboats. You could take all official Navy regulations and rules of conduct and just chuck them into the river. Boat crews could and did conduct themselves in any fashion they wanted, as long as they were ready for combat when an operation started. The standard uniform on our boat was solid green fatigue pants and shirt with no markings of rank and rarely tucked in, a couple of t-shirts, a jungle flop hat and a pair of home-made cut-off shorts, combat boots were only laced about a third of the way up (You'll understand why a bit later). On off days it was common to go shirtless with shorts and oh yea, flip flops. I did not cut my hair for the first 11 months and only did cut it when I went to Australia for R & R. The best part, I did not give one salute or use the word "sir" for nearly a full year. This Navy experience was surreal for sure but predictably I learned to love it, keeping in mind that life as I know it could end at any time.

This is the true, unfiltered raw and very personal story of two 19 year old sailors who were high school friends, and their transition to the dark side of the moon. One young man who transitioned from life to death and one who transitioned from the regular Navy, to unbelievable experiences that his young mind frequently could not comprehend, in the Mekong Delta of South Vietnam. This duty was not my father's spit and polish Navy but one of exceedingly long operational hours and the savage short-range firefights in enemy infested waters performed by the riverboat crews and the troops they transported.

Make no mistake, my tour of duty in Vietnam was dirty, hazardous, lonely, dangerous, tedious, exhausting and deadly, all at the same time. All done for an ungrateful American public and government. How many times can one fear for their life and continue to be effective in the job they were trained to do? How many of the enemy can you kill, and how many of your fellow sailors have to die or be mangled, before the mission is considered a success? How the hell are you supposed to function as a normal citizen if you do make it home? These are some of the questions I had before and while I was in Vietnam and sadly none of the questions were ever answered for me.

Vietnam had its own smell, its own feel, which I never got used to nor accepted. It was a place where the abnormal was normal and anything weird and outrageous could happen at any time. It was a place where my own government thought it was okay to dump deadly Agent Orange on its own troops under the auspices of, "What harm could it possibly cause?" There were days when I opened my eyes to a start new day and the first words that came out of my mouth were "What the fuck, I'm still here?" It was not a dream, I was still on the dark side of the moon. I have no regrets for my service in Vietnam and I'm extremely proud that I served my country, I only wish the government felt the same way about Vietnam combat veterans then and now.

CHAPTER 1

TRANSITIONS: VIETNAM STYLE

Doug Morton died in combat at age 20. He took a rocket propelled grenade to the head in Kien Hoa, South Vietnam on April 4th, 1968. He was 8 weeks into his tour of duty. He was just one of thousands of young American soldiers who remain, (other than to their families), nameless and forgotten.

Doug was from Phoenix, Arizona and we knew each other prior to going into the Navy. Our mothers actually worked together in retail. Doug and I joined the U.S. Navy at the same time, but after completing boot camp we were sent to different duty stations overseas. We did not hook up again until two years later at riverboat training in Vallejo, California. As it turned out we had both volunteered for gunboat duty at the same time, neither of us knew about the other's signing up.

Doug was no different than any other teenager from the 1960's and like a lot of those kids he thought that joining the military might help him decide what to do in life. Sadly there was only one focus for the military during this time and that was the growing conflict in South Vietnam.

Like me, Doug wanted more out of the Navy than just doing time on a boat or ship. We both had this hankering for a little adventure, a little something different that the average seaman's job. The Navy's "Brown Water" riverboats in the Delta of South Vietnam seemed to fit the bill. What we didn't know is that this strange world would cause transitions to take place in us that were not beneficial to either of us. Transitions Vietnam Style.

I cannot say that Doug and I were best friends prior to the Navy, but when I saw him In Vallejo, California just prior to riverboat training, I was excited that I actually saw somebody I knew from home. I think he felt the same way. We were young, very physically fit and ready for the challenge that lay ahead, regardless of the consequences. When you were young and naïve and in the hands of the US military you didn't think of consequences, any consequences, you just trained and got jacked up for the mission ahead.

I volunteered for the riverboats for two main reasons, I was then and am still very patriotic. Plus I was bored to death with the regular

Navy, especially with my duty station on the island of Guam. Guam, to put it very simply, just plain sucked. The locals hated Americans, so when we wanted to go ashore and into town we had to travel in packs to avoid the local thugs. As for meeting girls, forget about any chance with a local, it just wasn't going to happen. I had given some thought about making the Navy a career, but all of the rules and protocols were a turn off for me. My number one priority was to get off of that dumb-ass island and do something more adventurous, like maybe killing the enemy for my country. I was no hero. Just a sailor with an itch for action. I am sure Doug was the same way.

My firm belief is that the word "hero" is thrown around in today's society very loosely. The media refers to anyone who is currently serving in the Armed Forces as a hero, no matter if you are in a war zone or not. If you are in the line of fire and you jump in to drag two of your buddies to safety I believe this is your job and what you trained to do. This is what you are expected to do, it is your duty. I'm very old school and believe that all true heroes are deceased. They paid the ultimate price for their heroism by giving their lives, usually for a cause they thought was proper and right. It certainly takes courage to jump into the fire. Anyone who does that deserves a double pat on the back for their actions and a "job well done." Still, in my mind that is what you are supposed to do in that situation. I love and admire anyone who joins the military to serve their country, but heroes they are not. That title is reserved in my mind, for Doug Morton and all who did exactly what he did, fight like hell and let the chips fall where they may, God bless Doug Morton.

This is the story of *all* the Doug Morton's who fought, served and died in America's most unpopular conflict ever. It is the story about my experience and my way of honoring the thousands of combat troops who died like my friend Doug Morton, and who were unrecognized, at that time, by an ungrateful, even hostile country.

CHAPTER 2

MOBILE RIVERINE FORCE

The Navy had all types of boats and ships in and around South Vietnam and they all served a certain purpose or had a specific job to do. When I was stationed on Guam attached to a submarine tender, I would read the Stars and Stripes newspaper to see what was going on in the military and of course there were a ton of articles on the Vietnam War. I had seen a few articles on the Brown Water Navy which perked my interest and the Mobile Riverine Force (MRF) was just the ticket I was looking for.

The MRF was patterned after the French military model. They used boats to good effect in their war in Vietnam. The main purpose was to ferry combat troops into battle by navigating the hundreds of small rivers and canals that make up the Mekong Delta, going into places where tanks and ground troops could not gain access. For this same purpose the Navy and the Army partnered up using the Army's 9th Infantry Division for the combat troops. Navy crewman operating converted WWII landing craft were supported by armored gunboats (monitors), with one communication boat per division. The MRF was headquartered at Dong Tam in the Mekong Delta along with support or "mother ships" that were positioned on the Mekong River which were supposed to be able to be in close communication with the MRF's range of operations on the river. What they didn't tell you was that often we would be many miles from any support at all, as we cruised into this dense tangle of rivers and canals that meandered through thick, sweltering jungle. Each armored troop carrier (ATC) we escorted could carry a full infantry platoon. For firepower the boats were armed with a 20mm cannon, two .50 caliber machine guns and two Mark 18 grenade launchers, plus the crew's various hand held weapons. The ATCs not only landed troops, but also resupplied them and provided close-in fire support during operations. The MRF crews, except for the officers, were for the most part an all-volunteer effort and I did not think that you could actually get hurt or lose your life running these boats up and down these hundreds of small rivers. Still, none of that mattered to me, it was time to get off of the island of Guam and get into the fight. I spent the next 6 months filling out request forms called "chits" for a transfer to the MRF and finally got a reply of yes, *if* I would extend my service by 18 months. No problem, I got what I wanted. I gave no thought of how my request for transfer would affect my parents or family. However, I would discover all that later when I was able to go home just prior to shoving off for Vietnam. I could only hope to God I had made the right decision.

CHAPTER 3

TRAINING

After leaving Guam (thank God), and prior to the start of my training for the riverboats, I was given two weeks leave. So I went home to Phoenix to see my family. I was one of the few people in my family who had ever served in the military, so everything military to my family was foreign to them. Everybody knew by then that Vietnam was not a good thing. I think my parents were not only surprised that I volunteered for this dangerous duty, but that I had any interest in the war. They were wrong.

I didn't mince words and came right out and told them what was going on. My parents actually acted okay with the news. Still it was uncomfortable for me because I was ready to go, and the two weeks leave seemed to drag on forever. Now when I say my parents were okay with the news, well that is my interpretation of the story. In truth it killed my mom like it would any mother. I was 19 years old and had no clue on how a parent reacts to these things. The military at this time in history didn't want bleeding hearts and sissy boys for their war, they wanted guys like me who were ready for the challenge that lay ahead, I simply did not see the pain this caused my mother. I still think about that today.

The two weeks finally came to an end and I was on my way to Camp Pendleton for the first phase of the training. This was really weird for me because a few years earlier I was in San Diego for boot camp and now I found myself right back in the same place I started, kind of like going full circle. I'm not the sharpest tool in the shed and with a couple of years in the Navy under my belt I had been able to get exactly zero promotions and was still a lowly pay grade E-3. One notch above a brand new boot camp graduate. Still I was way ahead of the new crowd of students in my training class. I was 19 years old and tough as nails and easily breezed through the physical part of this training. This amounted to getting up early, putting on a heavy pack and getting screamed at all day by the instructors 'til late afternoon, doing the same thing all over again every day for a couple of weeks. Run, run, run, sweat, sweat, sweat, no big deal. I still had the ability to smoke a pack of very cheap cigarettes every day with no physical effects. But the best was yet to come.

I had never heard of SERE until the day we were on a bus headed to some remote part of the San Diego desert. It was a cold, November day in 1967 and I discovered that SERE stood for "Survival, Evasion, Resistance and Escape;" an advanced code-of-conduct course for military members in the event of capture by the enemy during combat. You know, what to do if you become a POW. *Captured by the enemy*, a Prisoner Of War, it never crossed my mind that this was a possibility. Now the gravity of the situation was starting to sink in. They were going to teach me how to survive in the wilderness if I was captured by the Viet Cong!

It turned out that we were heading for the SERE training center in the Cleveland National Forest, where there was a headquarters area with an administrative building, several staff barracks and a training compound. Training compound? No, it was actually a mock POW camp with barbed wire fences, and watch towers, with 24 hour a day high-powered search lights manned by the camp's staff scanning for escapees.

You know at first, when I heard the word camp it triggered great memories of my childhood with a week in the woods of Northern Arizona, riding horses, learning how to cook over a campfire, meeting new friends. This place was not a camp; it was a deadly serious reminder that if you did not listen and learn, it might cost you your life.

When we arrived at SERE our group was ushered into a large auditorium where we were greeted by a lone man dressed in civilian clothes. He commenced to inform us of what the program would consist of for the next week, two days of classroom instruction, and five days of, well let's just say *extensive survival training*.

Many official forms (with lot of pages I didn't care to read were passed out). I signed them all and passed them back in. The mood was pretty light and the first two days of class was rather a dull routine; learning such things as how to capture wild game, cleaning and cooking the same, surviving cold nights and days with the clothes you have on your back and other survival skills.

Day three began very early in the morning. All two hundred or so of the group were bussed to a very remote area of the desert, where we were introduced to a group of six or seven men all dressed in civilian clothes. We were given the following instructions; Everybody in the class was to spread out in a straight line spaced approx. 100 feet apart, we would then, on foot, head in the direction ordered for approximately 4 miles until we reached the "camp" (there's that fun word again!) There we would be given further instructions.

Like I have said before, I'm not the smartest guy in the world but I knew something was up. We were wearing standard issue green fatigues with no gear, nothing. No weapons, knives, shovels, packs, food or water and the weather was cloudy and cold. Now the hammer came down. We were told that we, as individuals had been separated from our unit behind enemy lines, we needed to go in the direction of the camp in order to hook up with our unit. A couple of miles ahead, the enemy has dispatched a platoon of armed men coming in our direction to find us before we could reach safety. We could not travel in pairs or teams, this is an individual exercise and we must work alone to reach our goal. There was only one rule. If we are captured we may call "time out" and proceed to tell our captor our brilliant plan to escape. If they liked our idea they could release us and we could continue on, if they did not like our idea we were instantly a POW and an ID number in black marker ink was put on the tops of our hand and we are hauled off, we were then officially declared POWs.

And just like that we were off. Some guys started in a full sprint, some at a fast walk and some just started walking like they were on a picnic. I really had no plan, the terrain was pretty rough and sparse, with only small shrubs and bushes, a few larger boulders here and there, but nothing really to hide behind. I decided to walk at a good pace and observe what was out in front of me, and react only when I thought I saw anything that might give me concern.

Two hundred plus people in one spot seems like it would be a crowded field, but in the open desert it took no time to find myself alone with nobody else in sight, which was fine with me. My course of action was simple, after about a mile in I decided to find the largest bush I could find and lay under it and simply wait it out. I had nothing to lose. I figured time was on my side. Besides, nobody said anything about a time limit, so that is what I did. I laid there for maybe an hour when suddenly I heard some commotion not too far away. I slowly rose up to see what I assume was the enemy. Two men in uniform with weapons, standing over one of the students and yelling for him to stand up. They were yelling in English but with some type of accent, maybe German.

The guy gets up off the ground and yells, "time out!" Okay, they asked, what is your escape plan? He stammers out, "Don't fuck with me, I'm a rock!" Out of character, both instructors laugh out loud and tell him good try, but suddenly back in character they scream at him, "You're fucked!" and marched him off towards the direction of the camp. I knew I was screwed and I was going to get captured. Besides it was getting close to sunset and I did not want to be out there alone at night. So I started to sprint towards the camp and within 5 minutes I was captured, a number was put on my hand and I was led to the camp.

I was actually stunned when I saw the POW camp for the first time, it looked like it was right out of the old TV show Hogan's Heroes. By which I mean it looked like a *real* German POW camp. I soon forgot that this was a training exercise and I was actually becoming uneasy with my surroundings. I don't remember if anybody made it to the camp successfully because my focus was on the stage that was set up in the middle of the camp yard. It wasn't like everybody was high-fiving each other after this exercise, the guards made it clear there would be no talking unless spoken to first. It was also made clear that we had better do what we were directed to do.

The group was marched into the yard directly in front of the stage and directed to stand at attention. Here's the weird thing, of all these men in the group and I had no idea who was an enlisted man, an officer or an aviator, because everybody was dressed the same and nobody in that class was emerging as a leader. It was clear to everybody that this was not a game, that these instructors were playing the part of the enemy and this was not going to be a walk in the park for the next five days. I knew that not everyone in the class was headed for the MRF like I was. I was almost sure there were more than Navy personnel attending, but I had no clue who was who or what was what.

We stood at attention in silence for a long of time. Finally a tall, white male, in maybe a German uniform, approached the center of the stage. He extended his arms towards us and in a European accent welcomed us to *his* camp. Now I'm creeped out. What the fuck is going on? It's cold out and I'm chilled to the bone, and some creep who looks like Colonel Klink is smiling at us from ear to ear. At this point I'm not sure what is really happening, I'm very cold to the point of shaking and some guy behind me is hacking and coughing, not a sick cough but a very nervous cough. I glance to my right and most of the group is

11

looking down towards the ground, there is a lot of tension in the air and I'm scared to death.

It was time to hear the rules of the camp, which were actually very simple. Rule #1. You were encouraged to escape from the camp, all successful escapees would receive a reward of one glass of cold milk and one ham and cheese sandwich, which the escapee would eat in front of the entire class. Rule #2. If you heard your I.D. number marked on your hand over the loudspeakers, you were to report at once to the shack on the far west side of the camp, day or night, 24-7. Rule #3. During daylight hours half of the group would leave the camp and forage for wild game in the desert and the other half would do labor inside the camp. All wild game caught would be brought back to camp and fixed as meals for everyone. Water would be provided, but anything to eat was the responsibility of the group, except of course, the ham sandwich provided by the camp commandant as a prize for a successful escape. That was it, those were the rules, obey or be punished.

By far the worst of situation up until then at the camp was twofold; the large Klieg lights that lit up the camp were left on all night long, making it hard to get any sleep. Then there was this constant blaring of Chinese music from the loudspeakers that ringed the camp, all day and all night, loud high pitched Chinese music.

Somebody's number would be called a few times an hour, day and night, and off they would go to report to the shack on the far west side of camp. It didn't take long to find out from those who returned that if your number was called it was your turn to be interrogated by the captors. The mood of the class was very low. There was not a lot of socializing amongst the class and again nobody was too excited to step up to the plate and become the leader. Everyone just appeared to be happy to lay low.

In the two days of classroom prior to us being bussed to the camp we were instructed on the proper protocol of answering any questions asked by your captors. We knew that name, rank and serial number were the only answers to be given, as well as to absolutely never sign anything on paper. But what if the captors wanted more from you, what then?

I'm sure I had heard the same numbers called on the PA system more than once, but nobody really knew what to expect when your number was up. Until late one night when the whole group was summoned before the camp commander in front of the stage. We all stood at attention. We could see that there was a single chair on the stage directly behind the commander. We watched until one member of the group was ushered to the chair by one of the guards. This guy looked horrible, it was obvious he had been crying and he was visibly shaking when they seated him. The commander looked back at him and asked if he was hungry and he nodded yes. The commander told him to speak up so the whole class could hear him. He looked up at us and stated, "Yes, I am hungry." At that point one of the guards brought out a ham sandwich and a glass of milk and handed it to the commander. With that I thought for sure this guy was one of the successful escapees and that he was brought here to collect his reward, but alas, I was wrong. The commander tells the class that this was a good boy who had cooperated with the guards. He said that in the interrogation session he went beyond the name rank and serial number routine, so he had been rewarded with food for his cooperation. He then instructed the student to eat the sandwich while the entire hungry, sleep deprived, chilled-to-the-bone group watched.

The kid had his head bowed down and started to cry uncontrollably while the commander handed him the sandwich and milk and instructed him to "Eat it *now!*" I had never seen anybody cry that hard and eat at the same time. While I was standing there watching this play out, it came to me that this was not some game we were playing, I felt sorry for the kid but at the same time I was furious that somebody on my team would sell the farm just so they could eat while the rest of us had to watch.

It took him 15 long minutes to down the milk and sandwich. When he was done the commander walked over to him and instructed him to tell the class that they too could have a sandwich and milk if only they would sign the form presented to them in the interrogation room, that there was no need to go hungry if we only did the right thing, like him. The kid fell to his knees and just cried and cried and then he was brutally dragged off the stage by the guards, never to be seen again. We were told at the very end of the week that he was washed out of the program and sent packing. This was the only time that a student who was washed out was put on display like this, but it really made me think I never wanted to be in that position. I was grateful it was not me

13

on that stage and I wanted no part of being a POW.

The last day arrived and my number had not been called yet. I was feeling confident I was going to make it through the week. I spent my last days moving rocks and stones from pile A to pile B and back again. I was on one "hunting" expedition where I think we caught one rabbit. Enough wild game and desert plants had been collected and prepared, so I was not feeling full, but I wasn't starving either. I smoked in those days. The only thing I was really craving was a cigarette, but so was everybody else. I had "rock" labor again that morning and just to change things up I moved the rocks from pile C to pile D but mostly I was just trying to stay under the radar. I briefly talked to four or five guys who had already been to interrogation. They had little to say. I assumed they were instructed not to talk about it so I didn't press them for answers.

I can tell you this, looking back on that morning of the last day of training, I truly was in this weird mental state of confusion. I had maybe got 2 or 2 ½ hours of sleep a night. I didn't take in enough calories in any 24 hour period to feel physically right. I stank to high heaven. I didn't trust the guys I had to sleep around. I was paranoid about my number being called while I was sleeping. And I wasn't really sure if the SERE course was either 3, 5, or 100 days long. I just simply forgot, but I was banking on 5 days.

It was almost noon and the Chinese music was burning a hole in my brain when it happened, I heard my number over the loudspeaker. I looked over my shoulder at the shack and I was like; "Crap, I don't want to go!" Somehow I get my feet to move in that direction and sprint over to the shack. The guard asks to see my number on my hand and then instructs me to go down the path, past the barracks 'til I see a round building with a courtyard in the middle. I was then to go to the courtyard and report to door number 4. I do as I'm told and have no problem finding the round building and I walk into the courtyard.

It is deadly quiet and there is no one there but me. I look around and there are probably 10 doors on the round building. As I get closer looking for door number 4, I see that all of the door numbers are in figures I don't recognize, like Asian numbers or figures. I can't tell one door number from the other! Since the building is in a circle with only one breezeway I don't know which side of the breezeway the numbers start from. I stand in silence for maybe 30 minutes just thinking that if I wait it out maybe all this will just go away. Of course nothing goes away and I decide to approach each door to see if the doors are opened or locked. I put my ear to them and try to determine if the rooms are empty or not. All ten doors are unlocked and the rooms appear empty. I'm thinking that somebody must be watching my movements. So as not to appear too stupid, I enter the door in front of me and enter the room. The room is cold. Approximately 10' X 20' with wooden floors, it is empty except for one desk and chair. It's so quiet inside I can no longer hear the Chinese music coming from the yard. I stand, not sit, struck with terror for maybe two hours when suddenly the door opens and I snap to attention and hold my breath.

If this exercise is make believe I cannot imagine what the real thing must be like. Just the unknowns of this whole experience has freaked me out. I'm 19 years old and going on 60. My mind was drawing a blank, how will I react to what's ahead, how will I respond to the pressure that is sure to come?

A middle-aged, white male enters the room, he is wearing some type of foreign military uniform. He is carrying a file in his right hand, he completely ignores me and sits at the desk, opens the file and starts to scan the forms inside. After a few minutes and without looking up he says; "Charles, please come over and face me." I comply. "Are you comfortable?" he asks. "Is there anything I can get you today?" Well now what? From what I understood the only reply you are to give to any question is the name, rank and serial number routine, so I make a snap decision . . . I do not reply to any questions for the duration. With that my heart rate jumps off the charts, but I stay at attention and focus my eyes on the wall behind the desk. I'm thinking in my current state of confusion and fear that if I answer any questions I might say or do something really stupid and I do not want to open another can of worms.

He looks up at me and repeats what he just asked. I do not move so much as a muscle. I try to stay focused. He slips out a piece of paper from the file and slides it and an ink pen across the desk in my direction and says; "I'm going to make this very easy for the both of us, simply sign the form that I have provided and you are free to go, no problems." I don't budge. I know I'm probably not the first guy to try the silent treatment on him. I know something bad is about to happen. Sure enough he stands up from the desk and walks around to my right side and coldcocks me with an open hand to the side of the head. I go down and decide to stay down but before I can think of what else to do, he grabs me by the throat, lifts me to my feet then slams me against the wall. We are eyeball to eyeball and he is squeezing my throat, I can smell his breath and he tells me that I'm a stupid boy and he releases his hand from my throat. My head is throbbing and my throat is bone dry. I couldn't talk now if I wanted to and I'm pretty sure I soiled my pants too.

He pulls me forward about 6 inches from the wall and tells me to get in a squatting position with my arms extended forward. "You stay in that position until I get back, don't you move!" and out the door he goes. The only positive thing about what just happened is that it only took less than 10 minutes to go down, no prolonged beatings or threats. Every moment is a lifetime when you're waiting for the healing to begin. I hold the position for no more than a minute and then I sit down. It was either that or fall down from fright, my legs felt like Jell-O anyway. At that moment in my life there is no way anybody could convince me that I was in the desert outside of San Diego in United States of America! My mind was twisted. I actually thought maybe I would not make it out of this place in one piece.

An hour or so later the door opens, I scramble to my feet. It is the same guy with two uniformed guards who stand by the door. He approaches me and tells me I have one more chance to sign the form before he is done with me and that he also has a nice, meaty sandwich waiting for me back in the yard; I have gone this far without speaking so I do not answer him. He once again body slams me against the wall and simply says; "You will die in this place!" I believe him and I fall to the floor. The two guards pick me up and start shoving me towards the door. I see it's almost dark outside and very cold. I have not had anything to eat or drink for hours. I fear the worst is yet to come.

The two guards escort me through the courtyard to the other side of the round building where we come to a well-lighted area with four or five guards all carrying black batons. On the ground there are five black boxes with lids of varying sizes. One of the guards throws a canteen of water at me and I slug it down. To say I was thirsty would be an understatement. The black boxes were spaced about five feet apart and all of them had holes drilled on all four sides with the end box the biggest. It was clear that two of the boxes were occupied, you could hear grunting and swearing coming from inside. The guards lead me to the biggest of the boxes and stands me in front of it. They order me to take off my boots, take my belt off and unbutton my pant buttons, which I do. My head is spinning, I have no clue what to make of these orders I'm following. Suddenly a guard on either side of me lifts me up by my arms and puts me in the box standing up. The box appears to be made of wood and measures approx. 4 foot tall by maybe 2 ½ to 3 feet wide, with an open lid. From the box the odor of urine and locker room sweat cuts through the cold night air and up my nostrils. I was obviously not the first poor guy to grace this box. I was ordered to cross my legs and to cross my arms across my chest and squat down so my head cleared the top of the box. Just as I reached that position the lid of the box came slamming down and I heard the click of a lock. I'm snug as a bug in a rug with very little wiggle room and locked down tight. I see rays of light streaming through the holes of the box and as I lay my hands on the bottom of the box for support I feel a cold, gooey liquid on the palms of my hands. It was a big, disgusting wad of mucus, a nice, big snot ball from the previous tenant. The guard bangs his baton on the side of the box and commands me to sound off, yell out my name and serial number. Then he moves on to the next box to repeat the command to my neighbor. I honestly do not know how long I was in the box. I hear the guard banging his baton on my box often. I respond with a loud cough, but I do not sound off. The more I cough the more he bangs his baton, insisting I yell out my name and serial number. My legs are cramping up and my body feels dead from the waist down. I can only move around inches at best and I try to close my eyes and sleep with no luck.

The only other "torture" device I was aware of at the camp was a large dunk-tank of water that I knew some guys were thrown in and were then forced underwater for a period of time. One guy told me later he was held under water repeatedly until he could not struggle any longer and they pulled him out. Apparently the water was ice cold and several feet deep. I prayed that wasn't coming next.

In the box my mind jumps from one thought to another and I wonder how it is that the instructors can be so physical with the group, isn't that some type of human rights violation? But this is the military and I bet myself that the papers they handed out the first day for us to sign had something to do with the physical part. I think that I must have blindly signed off and agreed to my own punishment.

I know now that it is late into the night and that I can hold on for only so long. I wonder if the kid who was forced to eat the sandwich in front of the class had been in this very same box. I wondered how long he held out before enough was enough and he signed his name on that form. I also think who would blame anybody for giving in? Maybe it was the wise thing to do? Just sign the fucking paper and be done with it. Still, hadn't I come down hard on that poor kid they forced to eat that sandwich on stage in front of us? Now I knew what he had gone through. Could I blame him?

I come to my senses and realize that what I'm going through right now is only a very small fraction of one percent of what a real POW must face daily. I muster up some balls and block all negative thoughts from my head and voila! The box's lid flies open and someone is screaming at me to stand up. My mind stands up but my body remains in the box. I can't even lift my head up to see out. These two guards continue to yell at me, banging their batons on either side of the box demanding that I stand up. I feel a hand under each armpit and up and out of the box I go, I land on my feet legs crossed, one of the guards reaches down and uncrosses my legs and both guards began to slap my legs with their batons. I really didn't feel any pain from the slapping. Actually, the longer they slapped the better my legs felt. I could feel the blood rushing back into my numbed legs. I was starting to feel stable when I was on my feet again.

I do not have any memory of what I was thinking at that exact moment, but it didn't matter because it was over, this was the last second of the SERE course for me. I was given water and the guards put a blanket around me, patted me on the back and escorted me out of the camp to a barracks that was supplied with a hot meal, hot showers and a clean bed. Most of my fellow classmates had made it to that barracks and the SERE course was officially done, over, no more.

The next day the class was assembled in a hall and it was time for a meet and greet. The entire SERE staff came on stage dressed in civilian clothes, each one introduced himself and gave a brief bio. It turned out that half of the staff were civilians and half active military. My guy from room #4 was a civilian and a former POW from WWII, (I actually got chills when he spoke and I was anxious to talk to him one on one). There were a few successful escapes from our camp and one guy escaped twice! A half dozen men like Ham Sandwich boy, were scrubbed from the program and sent back to their former duty stations. We were told that all in all we were a very successful class and they had hoped we had learned from this experience to avoid capture at any cost. If we were unsuccessful and did get caught by the enemy, use the lessons taught there to survive.

I did have a brief encounter with the #4 room guy. He told me that the silent treatment I used was probably not a good tactic because that type of behavior would probably attract too much attention to me and the end result would have not been good. Members of the group began to loosen up and everybody started to introduce themselves to each other. I learned that there were men from all branches of the service, every pay grade from E-3s, to aviators, to officers and even a couple of commanders. This was the first and last time in my military service that I was in such a mixed group of military men, all equal and with no chain of command barriers. In the end I was glad I was sent to this exercise. I think maybe this course, more than any other I took in the military, has stayed with me my whole life. It taught me that the mind is a powerful tool, that there is always someone else worse off than yourself. Most of all if you follow your instincts during times of need, you can survive and you can move forward.

After the SERE course we had another 3 ½ weeks of training in San Diego before heading north to Vallejo, California to complete the actual hands-on training for the riverboats. During that time my life took another kind of transition.

All through high school and after two years in the Navy I was still a virgin. This is something you do not brag about around veteran sailors. I was optimistic that things would change in that department soon. I had become pretty close pals with a guy from Sandy Hook, New Jersey and we started to hang out with a small group of other guys. I would normally go with him when we had liberty and just hang out around the San Diego area. Liberty was usually 12 hours long, so you could leave the base at 5:00 pm and be back no later than 5:00 am the next morning, though it was normally much earlier than 5:00 am because we had little money to spend.

On one liberty right after SERE, my New Jersey buddy and I scored a six pack of beer from some of-age sailors and went down to the beach. I saw two girls on a swing set and they caught our eye with a big smile, so we offered them a beer and we started to talk. One was a cute little blonde around 16 or 17 and the other her very overweight friend, who was attracted to my buddy. Soon the blonde invited us over to her apartment just off the beach and we drank the rest of the beers there. In no time my buddy takes the big girl into the only bedroom, leaving me alone with the blonde. She told me she was going to take a bath and asked me to unfold the sofa couch, and that she would be right back. I went into shock and panic mode and actually became *afraid* that my virginity was about to come to an end.

She called me from the bathroom. As I walked in she asks me to please wash her back with a wash cloth. This was the first time I had ever seen a fully naked girl in the flesh. I would have to say I liked what I saw, but I was so nervous that I quickly did what she asked and then rushed out of the bathroom. I went in and lay fully clothed on the bed staring at the ceiling when she came out of the bathroom and lay next to me naked. She was beautiful and everything I hoped she would be. She smelled fresh and clean, with a hint of perfume which was not like the smell of the barracks and the stench sweat and body odor which I was accustomed to. Instead of reaching for her . . . I was like a stick man and did not budge a muscle. She reached over and pulled off my clothes. Reading my body language she realized that I was a virgin. I was sweating bullets and extremely nervous. She asked me if I had ever been with a girl. I shook my head no. She gave a little laugh. She proceeded to rob me off my virginity . . . well it was more like me proudly giving it away.

The following 10 or 15 minutes were the best minutes in my short life. I think it must have been like someone taking heroin for the first time. I was overwhelmed and hooked. My buddy and I returned to the base, promising the two girls we would be back the following day. When the time arrived to go back though, my buddy tells me that I got the best end of the deal with the two girls and he was not interested in going back to their apartment. So I sprint back alone to her apartment. The blonde was disappointed that my buddy was not with me. She tells me unless I bring someone back with me for the big girl that we cannot have sex in the apartment. She says that she feels awkward that her friend had no one to be with. I promised her that I would bring someone with me, but when I returned to the base that afternoon my buddy had already spread the word that this girl he'd been with was really, really *big.* So nobody wanted to go with me to the girl's apartment.

When I got back the blonde said she understood. Still, she said that she had a favor to ask of me and if it worked out then bringing a friend back to the apartment would not be necessary. The blonde tells me that she is 16 years old and that in the state of California you must be 16 years and so many months old to get a driver's license . . . unless you are married. She said that she really needed a driver's license to get to work and she wanted to know if I would go to Vegas with her to get married. Then, when she gets her California license we get the marriage annulled before I get shipped up north.

I was so full of lust that I said something stupid like "sounds like a plan!" Then common sense and logistics kicked in. It was impossible for something like that to take place, as I was broke and did not have a car to drive to Vegas. Shortly thereafter we parted and I never saw the cute blonde girl again. In the end though, one major goal in my life was accomplished. I was no longer a virgin. And at the time that was a big deal to me. That at least was a natural transition from boyhood into manhood.

CHAPTER 4

MARE ISLAND VALLEJO, CALIFORNIA

By January of 1968 the United States had been involved one way or another in Vietnam for 3 years. After I left Vietnam in 1969 the war would continue on for another 7 years. When a green recruit becomes involved in any ongoing conflict, he finds that there are policies and customs in place when he arrives. For instance slang words used by the friendlies directed towards the enemy. It takes some time as a newbie to pick up on the verbiage used by the veterans. The slang used for the Viet Cong (VC) and the North Vietnamese Army (NVA) were the words "Charlie" or "Gook." These two words were used exclusively in referring to the enemy by everybody I was around, including the leaders and the officers. These names were in place when I arrived and continued to be used long after I left. Honestly, nobody I knew was offended by either name, by using them or hearing them. It appeared that if you were referring to the VC in general terms the name "Charlie" would be used, however "Gook" seemed to be used mostly in the field during times of stress, when things where hot and heavy. I only bring this up because the training I received at Mare Island was very intense, it was designed to save your life. I heard the word Gook from the instructors as often as I heard the F word from them. Gook appeared to be the aggressive name for both the NVA and the VC and of course I used it too. I know that this was not a "politically correct" way to refer to people, but I never heard the phrase "political correctness" until decades later, so it was no big deal at the time. You'll hear a lot of bad words in this story. Just remember these were different times.

Mare Island was a naval shipyard and base near Vallejo, California. This was to be our home for the next several weeks before heading to Vietnam. I was excited because they had actual working riverboats for us to train on and I was excited to learn all there was to know about them.

The training at Mare Island would also include weapons training, classroom work and of course a lot of physical training (PT), which started very early in the morning prior to breakfast. No problem for me. I actually liked the physical part of the training. We were housed in a two story barracks that had an open floor plan with single bunks and a locker for each man. It had one common head (bathroom), on each floor.

I had begun to form a bond with 6 or 7 of the guys and we set up in one corner of the barracks. We hung out there when not working. We were on the second floor of our building and actually it was quite comfortable. I had no problems with anything or anybody. I can tell you what I really liked though . . . Mare Island was like a regular job with no atmosphere of a boot camp or SERE training. It was like going back to being in the regular Navy.

For the most part we had a regular schedule for training with week-ends off. We were also allowed to leave the base at night on liberty. The base was large and had a PX (a kind of general store), laundry facilities, chow hall and all the things any other base had, and oh yeah, *a titty bar.* Can't remember the name of the "club" but there were no restrictions for visiting after work. That place became the number one destination for me and my buddies, as most of my pay went for beer and smokes. The dancers wore pasties and little outfits. The bar played loud western music and rock' n roll. For a small tip the dancers would dance on your tabletop. As long as you could answer the 4 AM bell every morning for PT, you could get as drunk as you liked. It was a huge difference from the first half of training and nobody I knew complained. The instructors expected and demanded that each member of the group give 100% while at Mare Island. This was no game. The real thing was fast approaching and everybody was aware of the deadly consequences if you did not take in what they were teaching you.

I believe the final headcount for the group was 188 men including Doug Morton who arrived at Mare Island a day or two after I did, I could not believe it when I saw him and it was so fantastic to know that we were going through this phase of training together.

I think all 188 of us had the same training in different locations prior to Mare Island and I believe Doug actually did his SERE training in the Philippines, but it didn't matter now, all of us would finish the training together there in Vallejo. I started to realize that this training had taught me one thing I didn't know about myself . . . and that was that I was one tough son of a bitch. I could be and was mentally and physically strong. I would support and respect all of my group in training and when we faced the enemy. I had started to form strong bonds with a few and I communicated effectively with everyone else. I liked where I was at in my own skin, which is a feeling I had never had in my life before. The thing I was really starting to love was that none of us were anything special; we were not the Green Beret's or Navy Seals, we were just a group of volunteers thrown together. We were starting to gel as a unit. We were becoming an actual combat force, and I was excited.

The majority of the topics in the classroom were the history of Vietnam as a country, Navy protocol in a war zone, and what to expect from your enemy. I always looked forward to the training in the field, the hands-on stuff that would be the key to daily success or failure of the mission. The class was split into groups of 20 to 30. You might do classroom a few hours, or for the entire day, it was always different. One class subject I will never forget and which actually played out several times during my tour was the class on Buddhist religion and what the Vietnamese believed about combat and life after death. I had believed in God all my life and feared death. Because of my religious beliefs I grew up in I knew I was going straight to hell. I prayed to God often but usually only when I wanted something really bad, the rest of the time I ignored Him. My family would not have approved of me smoking cigarettes, drinking mass quantities of beer, getting drunk and heading for the nearest tattoo shop, swearing like . . . well . . . like a drunken sailor and so forth. So I usually put the subject of God on the back burner and just did my own thing.

When I was home on leave with my family I laid low on the swearing and drinking, but one of my newly crafted tattoos on my upper right arm showed through my white t-shirt and my mother nearly fainted when she spotted it. You cannot explain away ink embedded into your arm, I tried unsuccessfully to calm my Mom. These were the times I knew my family did not understand me, when I felt like an outsider. I was anxious to get back to the Navy and get my training started. I was also sure that I was going to hell for ruining my mom's life. Back in class one day the instructor, by the show of hands, wanted to know who in the class would "go to hell if they died today?" Being a no-brainer for me I raised my hand along with 90% of the class and the instructor nodded his head and said that this was the big problem that we would face with Charlie. "You see," he says, "the gooks are taught from a very young age that if they die in combat they will go directly to Paradise, heaven awaits the warrior who prays to Buddha." "What does

24

this mean for you?" the instructor asks. "It means your enemy is not afraid to die but most of you are. In fact in some cases they would *rather die in combat* than go back to the poverty they came from. Which in turn means that your enemy will attempt to do anything it takes to kill you with no fear of dying."

I hadn't thought of that, but I understood the instructors point. If I was afraid to die, then I might be cowering in a corner someplace instead of fighting, and the enemy is fearlessly tracking me down to kill me. The instructor also tells us that in Charlie's belief system not only will he go to Paradise, but every member of his immediate family will follow him when they die! This is the way it is and you must remember that Charlie will not just go away, they are formidable opponent and they want to kill you.

I understood clearly what the instructor had taught us and this actually fell in line with my personal thoughts on the Vietnam conflict. Right or wrong the Americans were the invading occupying force of the country of Vietnam. The population should and would defend their country to the death. I should expect no less than one hell of a fight from them. After all, if the tables were turned on us we Americans would defend our land in the same way.

Bonding with my group, in my view, was an important part of the training. Bonding was defined as "hitting the titty bar." I'm guessing two nights during the work week and every week-end night "bonding" took place at the base nightclub. The club was actually very large and could serve probably a couple hundred men at a time. There was a juke box with all of the current 1960's hits and of course, my favorite thing, young girls my age, bouncing their pasty-clad titties around and dancing to the music. Prior to my military service I was what you would call a "shy person." I dated very rarely and only drank beer out of an A&W root beer can to hide the fact that I was drinking underage. So the interior of a bar was new to me. I did not know what a pasty was until I saw them worn on the nipples of the club dancers. I would have to say that I liked pasties.

So my group of guys would go to the club after work and gather around a table and the beer drinking would begin. Loud music with pretty girls wearing pasties was as good as it was going to get before our deployment and I didn't complain. It didn't take long for the dancers to realize that our group actually tipped more than most for their services. So they would come over to dance on our table as we whistled and acted out our male tribal instinct to act like asses.

There were basically two groups of men who patronized the club, the Brown Water Navy (us) and a division of US Marines who trained on the other side of the base. It doesn't take a military historian to know that mixing these two groups together while drinking alcohol may cause a flare-up or two. For the most part though it was usually peaceful . . . well like I said, *usually*.

I had never been in better physical condition in my life than now and I was proud of that. Proud to think that with mass quantities of beer for fuel I could do and say things that I might not do or say when I was judiciously sober.

So on one particular weekend night it was very close to closing time and I stumbled to the can to take a leak. I'm standing at the urinal and a very drunk Marine pulls into the urinal next to me and we make eye contact. I'm still not sure to this day why I did what I did, but I did it without hesitation! I cold-cocked him on the side of the head and we both go down to the deck in a serious struggle. Sadly for me four of his Marine buddies had entered the can and it became a free for all on me. I was taking a pretty good licking when I was rescued by four or so of my pals who had come to check on me. It became an honest to goodness military bar-brawl right there in the club head.

Within in minutes I hear the siren of a MP jeep and everybody scrambles to get out of the club except me and the guy I cold-cocked, we continued to tussle until the MP's broke it up. I was banged up pretty good but less than the Marine. At that moment I knew I was ready to get it on. Let's get this party started and get to Vietnam. I had found my manhood in that bathroom and I was proud of myself, whether that was right or wrong, I don't know. The Marine and I were both cited, but we weren't sent to the brig. I was ordered to Captain's Mast (military court) in the near future to learn my punishment for the fight. Still, I was a proud sailor that night and I was treated like a hero by my pals back at the barracks.

When fully engorged with beer, one of the favorite drinking games at our table was to take a combat boot from a volunteer and start to pass it along from person to person and drop or pour whatever you wanted into the boot. This might be a full ashtray, beer, hard liquor, food scraps and in one case the lipstick from one of the dancers. I, along with others, donated spit to the boot. Soon the boot was full. It was then shaken like a cocktail and passed around the table for all to drink from. To describe the bouquet of this bonding cocktail would probably vary from man to man. My take on the taste would be to say it was like a fine wine or brandy and simply great . . . that's a lie.

In my defense I was drunk when this all went down, but being drunk did not hide or change the taste of the drink. Imagine going to your favorite sports bar and getting on your hands and knees between the tables and began to lick everything in your path with your tongue. The floor may have deposits of food and sauces, body fluids, whatever can be tracked in on the bottom of dozens of shoes, dirty and soiled napkins, well you get the picture. Now imagine how that would taste on your pallet, this is how the bonding cocktail tasted to me.

An explanation of the boot is in order, this is a combat boot worn by a combat enlistee who had trained for weeks in all types of weather conditions and temperatures. The word "salty" was kindly used to describe the condition and the smell of the boot. We were all happy and honored to drink from the boot until it was emptied. Bonding is not a strong enough of a word to describe this experience, though bonding it was. I was proud of myself and the men I trained with. The boot drinking was the seal of approval on all those feelings. It is something to be 19 years of age and to be molded into something you never thought was possible . . . a man. This was another transition, Vietnam style. You just had to experience something like this yourself to truly understand it. It created a brotherhood that could not be broken even in the toughest times of combat, I promise you that.

This experience may gross out some, even appearing immature or dysfunctional to others. In reality this game we played was nowhere close to the experiences that were to come when we entered combat on the dark side of the moon. The training and all of the antics that went along with it was simply child's play, a way to bury the anxiety that was burning inside of me.

My buddy from Sandy Hook, New Jersey came to me one night and asked me what I was doing that coming week-end. I said probably the usual and I asked why. He said that he was considering getting on a plane and flying home to New Jersey and wanted to know if I wanted to tag along. There were a couple of problems with his plan. The first thing was that our week-end liberty was only 72 hours in length. The second thing was I had no money for a round trip to New Jersey, not that I wouldn't go if I had the chance. I knew that his family was wealthy. He said they would pay for the trip for both of us. He said his family would do anything to see him one more time before we deployed to Vietnam, but they did not want him to travel alone.

My next thought was that this was payback of some kind or a trick to get back at me for the "big girl" incident in San Diego. Maybe he has something up his sleeve to get back at me. He tells me this is no joke. So my question to him was how do we fly round trip, coast to coast and get back in time for Monday morning? He reminds me that we had that coming Friday off from class, so we could fly off the first flight early Friday morning and arrive back late Sunday night, even make it back in time for Monday morning PT. He said his family had the plane tickets ready to go and he wanted to know if I was in or out, I tell him, "Fuckin' A I'm in!"

My only real concern was that when arriving at the airport we would need to show some type of ID to get the tickets. I didn't even have a driver's license to show, only a military picture ID and the 72 hour green ID pass issued by the Navy. If we got caught getting on an airplane and violating the rules we would be in big trouble. I believe the maximum distance we could travel on liberty was only 50 miles. So we were taking a big gamble.

We got to the airport, showed our military ID's and low and behold, we boarded the plane and took off for the East Coast, no problem. I had never been to New York and my friend would take the lead and get us there and back safely and quickly. I trusted my friend, he was born and raised in Jersey and he knew how to get around the quickest way possible. We landed in New York, took a cab to the Port Authority Bus Terminal and caught a bus to Sandy Hook. All I really remember now was that New York City was way bigger than I thought it might be, and that my buddy had a couple of really cute sisters. We spent our time with his family and then caught a flight back to California. We made it in time for physical training Monday morning, we never told anybody in the group about the trip and I was very pleased that we actually pulled it off.

After the trip to New Jersey and close to our departure date to Vietnam, I was brought up in front the "Old Man" at Captain's Mast, to hear my punishment for the club fight. I was only an E-3 enlisted man and a drop in pay grade to an E-2 was about the only thing I could imagine I would get and I was correct. O.K., I'm now a proud E-2. The biggest blow was that the Old Man ordered me to shave my hair, just like in boot camp. I loved my full locks of hair and the haircut was a bigger blow to me than the demotion. Still, I took it like a man and moved on.

Usually once a week-end I made a trip to the base PX to buy some personal items. Since my experience with the blonde in San Diego all I could think about was sex and more sex. There was a really cute female employee at the PX that caught my eye and I always went out of my way to say "hey" to her. I remembered her last name, her married last name, but not her first name. To my surprise she responded to my flirting and we talked a little more each time I went in. I learned she lived off base in a small, one bedroom apartment not far from the main gate. Her husband was a marine in Vietnam and she took the PX job to help pay the bills and fight the boredom. She made it clear to me she was lonely and missed her marine greatly.

To be very clear, at this point in my life I loved and craved sex. That little blonde in San Diego really put a hex on me. So having a very attractive female respond favorably to me was unusual but totally cool. I think that this girl missed sex with her husband and just needed to be with a man. Yet, like a programmed robot I followed her lead willingly. One week-end night I found myself at her apartment and I followed her lead a little farther. One thing led to another and the deed was done.

Most 19 year old kids in my position would have been elated and bragged about the conquest, but there was something very sad about the whole experience as she talked about her husband in the past tense . . . like she really did not expect him to survive Vietnam. Even though he was a marine I felt like I had betrayed a fellow combatant by seducing his wife. I spent the night with her, went back to the base and I never saw her again. I felt a great remorse for what I did. It took me a while to shake that feeling of cheating on a fellow combatant.

Just outside of the main gate of the base was a small liquor store and my group discovered that you could buy a gallon jug of California Red Mountain wine for $1.10. Even poor guys like us could afford that. So Red Mountain wine became the official liquid libation of the group while at the base.

We were very close to the end of training at Mare Island. Our excitement was growing. We had no fear yet. Though we did have a vague, disquieting sense about the "unknown" that lay ahead of us. The nighttime drinking and partying continued. That activity barely caused a blip in the daily physical training we endured.

I was in top shape and felt I could take anything that was thrown at me. I got so drunk one evening I decided to go outside of the barracks in the rain to test my manhood by telling another guy to hit me as hard as he could in my face. He did it! My nose was driven to the left side of my face and blood gushed out of my nose as I staggered into the head, I took a look in the mirror to check out the damage. The only thing I could do was smile back at myself, I was (to my mind) totally ready now for bigger and meaner things.

The Red Mountain wine drinking marathons had become legendary. However they did cause a concern when the base commanders cracked down on the whole group with only a week of training to go. All off-base passes and club visitations were cancelled, and lights out was pushed ahead by a couple of hours. This caused a major concern for the group. However we did find a work-around. With no help from me, many gallons of Red Mountain wine were somehow stored away in our barracks and there was plenty to go around for all. A mystery for sure.

The last week of training was uneventful and the day of our departure finally arrived. The mood of the group was good but the base brass were not taking any chances. All of our sea-bags were loosely inspected for contraband (i.e., Red Mountain wine), prior to loading us on the busses. As I filed onto the bus with the others I was thinking that a swig out of the wine jug sounded pretty good. Everybody was on their best behavior while waiting to depart and I could see out of the bus window that the brass were lined up, eagerly waiting for us to go.

I was told that while our group was on the base that we racked up a ton of Captain's Masts for misbehavior and that we actually set some type of record for numbers of Masts attended. So I'm guessing the brass felt that a good riddance to us was in order. As the busses slowly began to roll out of the base I heard a commotion in the back of my bus, I looked back and a gallon of Red Mountain wine was making its way forward for all to partake in, God I loved this group!

CHAPTER 5

JANUARY, 1968: TET OFFENSIVE

On January 26th we flew Flying Tigers Airline from California to Okinawa for a fueling stop before touching down in Saigon. The plans changed when it was learned that there was some type of major action going on in or around our destination point of Tan Son Nhut Air Base in Saigon. We laid over for two nights in Okinawa. The group was issued a few bucks from our pay and we were allowed to go on base and see the sights, well see the base club anyway.

As an E-2 in 1968 my salary in the Navy was approx. $180.00 a month. But I got a combat pay raise of $60.00 on top of that, so I was making the grand total of $240.00 a month while on tour in Vietnam. However, I did learn later that as soon as we got in-country I was to be promoted back to an E-3. This meant that I had an extra $30.00 or so more added to my pay. Looking back, the two extra days waiting on Okinawa was not a good thing, it simply ramped up the anxiety levels, as the whole group was anxious to get there and get started.

On January 29th, 1968 the 188 men in my group lifted off from Okinawa and we headed for Vietnam. I remember the mood was pretty good and there was a loud raucous singing of the "Vietnam Song" by Country Joe and the Fish; ". . . And its 1, 2, 3 what are we fightin' for? Don't ask me I don't give a damn, the next stop is Vietnam, and its 5, 6, 7 open up the pearly gates. Well there ain't no time to wonder why . . . WHOOPEE we're all gonna die!" Now that's some funny stuff.

An hour or so out from landing, the Flying Tigers Airlines Captain came on and told us that there was some "activity" on the runway at Tan Son Nhut. He said that he was going to take an evasive "dive-bomb" approach for landing at the base! No singing now. It is quiet as can be as this news sinks in, not only was it going to make a dive-bomb approach to the runway, but the plane was not going to shut down after landing. It would sit on the runway, unload us ASAP and proceed to takeoff immediately. We hadn't hit the ground yet and we're in the middle of a shit storm. Open up the pearly gates, *WHOOPEE we're all gonna die!*

In short order the plane descended and I got my first glimpse out the window of Vietnam. This was the first feeling of fear that had come

31

over me since this experience started. My home for the next 12 months lay beneath me. It was a real war-zone. I realized I might not make it twelve minutes, let alone twelve months. I actually felt ill not only in my physical body but also in my soul as I was afraid to die. I mean, I thought I was a good person, but the way I was raised . . . I knew if I so much as fantasized about having sex with a girl, I would go to hell. It is slowly sinking in that the land below me could be the place I would die and I was scared to death of going to hell.

The plane now began a very steep decent on its final approach. As the runway came into view I saw bunkers on our side of the runway, manned by soldiers firing their weapons into the surrounding brush and trees. There was a full-fledged firefight going on as we landed! The cabin crew hustled to the back of the plane as the plane came to an abrupt stop with the engines whining at full speed. A jeep with an airplane ladder attached sped toward the plane, the door flew open and we were ordered to disembark single file and run across the open runway to the terminal. "Shit!" I say to myself as my turn comes. I hustled down the ladder and I started to sprint towards the terminal. I briefly look back at the plane and I see a crew of men frantically unloading our sea-bags from the plane and I think something to the effect of; "Well fuck me!"

Organized chaos ensued inside the terminal as we were still under attack and night was quickly coming on. None of the group had any personal weapons issued yet, so we felt like that old sitting duck, just waiting for something bad to happen. The decision was made that we spend the night in the terminal and try to resume the processing schedule early in the morning. The base was heavily defended and we were assured that we were safer there than somewhere else that night. I was scared, hungry and could not sleep. During the night I could hear sounds of gun fire and mortar fire outside of the terminal and see the night sky lighting up with flares. What a hell of an introduction to Vietnam! Apparently the TET Offensive was on the starting blocks. The TET offensive was a military campaign that was launched on January 30, 1968 by regular and irregular forces of the People's Army of Vietnam. The offensive was to use the element of surprise and strike military and civilians throughout South Vietnam without mercy. This was scheduled during a period when no attacks were supposed take place because of Lunar New Year Celebrations, a holy festival that all Vietnamese, North and South supposedly respected. I could see we were fighting an enemy that respected nothing and would do anything to win this war.

So my first day in-country was on the eve of TET. There was massive combat activity surrounding the terminal and we were just trying to get processed in, and if nothing else, at least be assigned a personal weapon so we could have some sense of protection. I asked for this duty, I trained for this duty and now the reality was staring me in the face, "go big or go home" was the attitude I decided to take.

The next morning's plan was simple, get bussed to a local compound to be processed in, then load onto choppers to be transported to Dong Tam, south of Saigon, the home of the Mobile Riverine Force. In the morning the group was loaded onto busses. As we pulled away from the terminal we saw a half dozen dead VC lying on the ground from the previous night's firefight. Each dead VC was wearing a vest of explosives around their chests. We were told that these were elite commandos trying to breech the airport terminal. This was the first time in my young life that I had seen actual dead bodies and they were spread out on the lawn of the terminal like giant chess game pieces that you might see at a fancy resort hotel. I was horrified by what I saw and I think I actually looked away from this sight in order to gather my composure.

We were taken to an old three or four story hotel and ushered inside for processing. We were now in the Cholon (Chinese) District of Saigon and there was much activity all around us: helicopter gunships, tanks, troop transports, a whole lot of noise and billowing black smoke in every direction.

The processing took a few days to complete and we were required to stay in our rooms and only leave for chow, which was in the building next to us. There was a lot of speculation amongst the group about what was going on around us, but it is clear the VC were extremely active in the area and the TET Offensive was in high gear.

Since TET was a complete surprise to the military, a smooth processing for us appeared unlikely. We were told that the Navy was scrambling to complete this process as fast as possible and to get us down to the Delta quickly. All available military equipment in the Saigon area was being utilized to suppress the TET Offensive, so we might be in Saigon longer than planned.

The group's first KIA (Killed In Action) causality was on our second day at the hotel, when one of the men was walking between the two buildings going for dinner. He was killed by a sniper's bullet. I can't say I was stunned by this event, but it really brought this conflict close to home and I wanted out of Saigon badly. I felt we did not have a fighting chance cooped up in a hotel room with no weapons. I had been in-country for 48 hours and I could not believe what I had witnessed in such a short amount of time. I look down at the street below my room and I witness a speeding armored tank run over and crush a civilian on a bicycle! It just kept moving down the road, I can't even tell you if it was an American or ARVN tank. It was all in slow motion and reminded me of a cheaply made Hollywood movie stunt. My lily-white ass' 19 year old brain could not begin to compute what was going on and I was extremely scared.

Finally the processing was over on the morning of the 4th day of January. The first seven or eight guys loaded on the first chopper out heading south; when word came back only a few minutes later that the bird had been shot down and all aboard had perished! This intel brought an abrupt halt to the use of choppers for transporting to Dong Tam, it was simply too dangerous to transport that way. The plan was changed to transporting the whole group together by ship. In-country for only a few days and seven or so of my original group is already dead, not killed in a firefight, but killed by simply moving around trying to get to the boats.

The rest of us loaded onto a large support ship and we made our way down river to Dong Tam. After a full day we were in the heart of the Mekong Delta; a hot, muggy, big batch of canals, rivers and streams surrounded by a thick, triple canopy jungle. This was the reason the Mobile Riverine Force was created, to access areas that tanks and tracked vehicles could not penetrate, to crawl up the small, winding canals and estuaries in search of the enemy. We were to find and destroy bunker complexes and enemy command bases that normal Army platoons could not reach.

Staring out over the landscape from the deck of the transport ship I thought that this is an impossible task which we were about to take on. Hunting down the gooks on their home field, in weather that was unpredictable, using old converted WWII landing craft. My thought was if you did take some ground from the VC, how in the hell do you keep it? After all we are called the *Mobile* Riverine Force and we would be constantly on the move. How do you capture a piece of the river when you don't stick around long enough to hold on to it? These were the questions that I knew would be answered in a short time. I was extremely anxious to be assigned to a boat and crew, and to find out what this was all about.

CHAPTER 6

DONG TAM, SOUTH VIETNAM

We arrived at this sprawling base in the middle of the Mekong Delta which was Dong Tam, the home of the Mobile Riverine Force as well as a brigade of the Army's Ninth Infantry Division. Dong Tam was responsible for fuel, ammunition, supplies, maintenance and repair of river craft. It also facilitated boat berthing, dry docking, communications and the sleeping and mess facilities for the river assault squadrons.

TET was well underway and there was this palpable sense of concern from just about everybody. The VC had ramped up their efforts and Dong Tam was a *very big* target. We were ushered into a group of barracks to wait for our boat assignments. The first night there was some activity on the perimeter of the base and I along with others were ordered to a bunker. I was finally given an M-16 rifle, but told not to fire unless ordered to. I could hear small arms fire cracking and popping in the distance. We mostly sat in the bunker, scared shitless. I'm thinking it's a bad dream about being hunkered down in a bunker in Vietnam waiting for the gooks to invade this base. I was with a few other sailors who were from my group. Mostly it is five or six Army guys who are not talking and appear to be taking all of this gloom and doom in stride. I think to myself how the fuck can you peer out into the darkness and not show any emotion? Maybe for them this is a cake walk but I'm a million miles from home. I could not see clearly past my own nose from the stinging sweat seeping into my eyes. I don't think this nightmare duty was in my job description.

It's strange how when you see and experience things that are strikingly harsh, it seems like a dream. Must be a sort of defense mechanism. I'd already seen a shit-load of death and destruction in the past week. But each episode just didn't seem real. It was like my mind just couldn't accept it.

Sunrise arrives with no attack and we head back to the barracks. There had been no physical harm but my nerves were frayed and I still had 11 months and 3 weeks to go on my tour.

Dong Tam was the base of operations, yet I had no idea how they picked the boat or crew I would be assigned to. I had only been in-country less than a week and I was already mentally weary, mostly from

36

the lack of solid, uninterrupted sleep. Finally I was assigned to the command and communications boat C-112-1, River Assault Division 11. We had a six man crew and the boat captain. I knew all five guys on the boat, but not the captain. My friend Doug Morton was assigned to monitor boat M-91-3 in a different River Assault Division, sadly I rarely saw him after that day. We had pretty much been through this insane couple of weeks together. Now we were separated and that felt bad.

The communication boat was different than the other boats in the squadron. When on the river, the officer in charge was on the CCB directing all aspects of the operation, we carried no combat troops. The 60 foot boat was fitted with an array of high-tech (for the day), radios and transceivers in the command center. It was armed with a 40mm cannon turret on the bow, two 20mm cannon turrets on the aft, small arms and mortars of all sizes. The CCB was positioned in the middle of the convoy and was easy to spot because of the large numbers painted on the side and the four, long communication whip antennas that graced the top of the boat. There were a couple of bunks positioned in the command center and we slept in shifts of two. The quarters were slightly tight but livable. In the mid-section of the boat, behind the communication center, was a row of small lockers, storage bins and areas to hold water, combat rations and miscellaneous ammunition.

The one thing that crossed my mind when I was assigned to the CCB was that I knew from class and common sense that you always go after your enemy's communication systems first, cut off their ability to communicate. I look at the CCB and I see these long antennas on the top and the big C painted in bright white paint on the side of the boat and I think maybe this boat screams out; "Here I am! I'm the communications boat! Kick my ass first!" Or maybe I was just being paranoid? I was sure I would find out soon.

The previous crew of the CCB had already departed when we boarded, which was a shame as I wanted to pick their brains on anything that might help this green crew survive our first operation. So with no help at all we tried to settle in as best we could. The first impression I had of C-112-1 when I boarded her for the first time was how does this big tub get any speed? The boat was a big pile of steel armor and not very stealthy looking. The interior smelled of stale cigarettes and of man sweat, not the type of atmosphere for a good night's sleep, which I was craving. I asked the coxswain what the top speed of this beast was and he said maybe 8 or 9 knots and I think "were fucked," no speed for a quick exit.

The boat crew's age ranged from 19 to 23 years of age. The captain was a career Navy man who was probably 35 years old but looked 55. He had a slight build, gray hair and a scruffy thin white beard. I had never seen him before, none of the crew knew where he had come from and he had not trained with us.

There was no immediate connection between him and us. The first week or so he stayed to himself and only spoke when he was giving directives. None of us, including the captain, had ever seen combat. So it was kind of like the blind-leading-the-blind. Still, I figured we were well trained and ready to test the fires.

Each riverboat in the division was a commissioned boat or ship of the United States Navy, flying the American flag, like every other ship in the U.S. Navy fleet worldwide. The boat's captain had as much authority as any other captain of any other ship in the Navy. Our crew understood this and we all gave him that respect. His orders were carried out by the entire crew with no questions asked. This was about as much Navy tradition as I would see my entire tour on the rivers. As it turned out, this captain was not discipline driven. As long as you did your assigned job, there were no problems with him and every man on our crew did their job.

A typical operation for the river boats went something like this: ATCs (Armored Troop Carriers, nicknamed 'Tangos'), were loaded with one platoon of combat soldiers from the Army's 9th Infantry Division. They were escorted to their objective by the Monitor boats, which were the boats with the fire power. Sometimes the convoy was escorted by ASPB's which were lighter in weight and could maneuver quicker than the troop carriers or the monitors. Of course the CCB was in the middle of the pack.

There might be as many as 15 to 30 boats in the convoy on any given operation. If, from point A to point B, the convoy made enemy contact, the policy of the MRF was to turn into the firefight and drop the troops where the fire was coming from and engage the enemy. As it turned out this was a very common practice.

All of the troop carrying boats were converted WWII LCM (landing craft) with quarter inch armored plating with added rebar in many areas to trigger any rockets to blow before they hit a critical part of the boat. They were very heavy in weight at about 66 tons, powered by two Detroit diesel marine engines. The boats could lumber along at maybe 8 knots top speed. If you were fighting the river current they were even slower. There was plenty of rebar armor placed near the wheelhouse to protect the coxswain from RPGs. Rebar was also placed near and around the mid-section of the boat to protect the command center. Above the coxswain wheelhouse, squeezed between the two 20mm cannon turrets, was a small plastic seat that the boat captain sat in to direct the operation of the boat during firefights. The captain wore a radio headset and could communicate directly with the crew of the 40mm cannon on the bow, or the two 20mm turrets on the aft to direct their line of fire towards the enemy. From where the captain sat he had a clear line of sight of what was in front of the riverboat and could easily give direction to the cannon crew. The officer in charge of the operation might stay below in the command center or take the place of the boat captain at his post in the chair. The officers in charge were usually an Army officers of varying grades. Sometimes we were graced by the presence of Commander R.H. Sullivan of the US Navy, who was a colorful character all by himself.

So this is how it was. We were ready to go out on our first operation as soon as the boat captain assigned us our duty stations. The coxswain position was assigned to a crewman who had been trained to steer this mammoth beast back in Vallejo. I was initially assigned as a 20mm gunner and later assigned to the 40mm turret. The rest of the crew got their posts assigned to the other stations. The captain for some reason remained pretty aloof around the crew. Maybe it was just nerves, or maybe he was scared as hell like the rest of us.

CHAPTER 7

OPERATING IN THE MEKONG DELTA, SOUTH VIETNAM

Military Zone IV Corp was the Mekong Delta in South Vietnam. This was the operating area of the MRF where I spent the majority of my time in-country. Before going on my first operation I got some good, solid advice from a departing Brown Water sailor who was heading "back to the world." First tip was to never lace your combat boots to the top eyes but only to mid-boot so the boots fit loosely. It seemed that there were two high and two low tides daily on the rivers and canals of the delta. The water level might rise 8 to 10 feet depending on the tides. The river currents were some of the swiftest in the world, meaning that if you found yourself in the river for any reason you needed to be able to kick off your boots to avoid drowning. Second, if you were unlucky enough to be assigned to the 40mm cannon crew you had to know a few things. The 40mm gun turret was a fully enclosed ¼" thick steel box with no ventilation, with only one very small hatch to enter and exit. The inside of the turret was smelly, muggy and hot as hell. Sitting there for long stretches of time became almost unbearable, at the same time you had to be ready to load the cannon if contact was made with the VC. Sitting on the hard steel of the cannon for hours at a time became a real problem for my ass. It did not take me long to figure out that I needed a cushion to sit on so I took an unused flak jacket and draped it over the top of the canon, if your ass is happy than you are happy and the flak jacket worked out great.

The weather was normally hot and humid, so you needed to drink massive amounts of water to stay hydrated. Inside the turret you wore your flak-jacket over your bare skin so your sweat could be absorbed into the flak-jacket. The sailor said this would keep you cooler and add density to the flak -jacket. Third tip was to keep your feet dry and aired out daily. If your feet got wet from the river water or sweat you could pick up a fungus. Then your feet and toenails became infected, this was called "Jungle Rot" and it was no joke. The last bit of knowledge I was given was that the command boat would normally be hit by rocket fire first. That would signal the beginning of a firefight which confirmed my earlier suspicions about the vulnerability of a CCB.

The first order of business for me was to figure out the simple things of life on the boat, like taking a piss or having a bowel movement. When do you eat and what is there to eat? How does the sleeping rotation work? I quickly found out that this assignment was not like the regular Navy I was accustomed to when it came to hygiene, uniforms and personal grooming. This is how it worked: the pissing part was easy, just do it in the river, got a bowel movement? Take a bucket on a rope, dip it in the river and fill it half full and cop a squat. I had maybe 5 Navy issued t-shirts and 3 pairs of issued trousers, 1 pair of homemade cut-off shorts and 1 pair of jungle combat boots in my sea bag. That is all I would need for the entire tour. You just washed them in the river and let them hang dry. Showering while on an operation was another story, it didn't happen. When the heavy monsoon rains came, you could go buck naked with a bar of soap and get stupidly clean quick, so that is what I did. Pre and post operations hot showers and a hot meal were available on the support ships, the rest of the time you made-do. Maybe it was just our boat but our crew paid little attention to Navy regulations and we did not concern ourselves with beard or haircut regulations, or uniform requirements. The boat captain did not appear to care either. After 11 months into my tour I had not had a haircut. I hid my hair length under camouflage flop hats. I even went to sleep with the hat pulled over my ears. After being demoted and having my head shaved stateside I had no intention of letting them crop my head again.

The basic daily meal was combat rations in a can. In the beginning of my tour Korean war era c-rats were still in use but happily after a short time they were all used up. My favorite meal was the pound cake and peanut butter. Occasionally I would eat the spaghetti or some other meal provided but I relied heavily on the peanut butter to get me through most of the time.

The operational routine for the Army was very basic, load onto the riverboats in full battle gear, head up the small rivers and canals of the Mekong Delta and wait for Charlie to make the first move. The operations could last a couple of days, or as long as a week or two. I think the criteria for the length of the mission was how much contact you might make with Charlie. The more contact made, the more aggressive the operation became. There were always helicopter gunships in the area we operated. If the enemy contact was heavy the choppers were called in to assist in the firefights. The term used in 1968 was "seek and destroy" when chasing Charlie into the dense, green jungle. Honestly I think some operations there was no destination or end point in mind, just head up the river with a convoy of boats and see what happens, like throwing something on a wall and see what sticks. After every firefight the Army would do a sweep of the area and collect anything left behind by Charlie including bodies. The enemy, I was told, did a good job of collecting their dead, so an accurate number of actual Charlie KIA's might be difficult to measure if we let them take their bodies away.

As my tour ground on, the sight of so many dead VC affected me very little, but I was interested in the numbers that the Army would declare as KIA in any action. I would witness maybe 10 or so dead VC after a firefight but somehow the number the Army released was usually 40 or 50. I quickly learned that this war was a numbers game and the more you claimed killed, the better things looked to others who were keeping the tally someplace else. This was going to be a dirty business and I decided to just play stupid and do my job, which was to do what I was told, survive any way I could and go home alive in one piece.

Before I arrived on the boats the Army did a sweep after a good sized firefight. They found an article from a popular American magazine featuring the MRF in the pocket of one dead VC. The article showed photos, drawings and diagrams of the boats conversion from WWII craft. It detailed where the troops sat in the well of the boats, the gun placements on the boats, the engine and communication placements and how many crew were on the different types of boats used in the MRF! This information made it fairly easy for the enemy to place an RPG7 or B40 rocket into every place that could cause the most extreme damage to life and equipment on the boats. All Charlie had to do was just zero in on the diagrams in the magazine article. A well placed rocket or two into the well of a troop carrier could easily take out the majority of troops, and the same for any of the turrets on the boats. I thought to myself that the deck was stacked against the MRF on these operations. In the end I was still anxious to get the first firefight under my belt.

When the first orders for an operation utilizing our CCB and its new crew had finally come through, I had no idea what to expect, but I was game and ready for the challenge. In all of the operations I was involved in I never once knew what our destination was or how long we would be out. It was like a game of follow the leader and I just went along for the ride.

I was not really nervous, but after hours of moving up a river we turned into a small complex of canals. I was surprised how narrow the canal was and how it was lined on either side with thick, jungle canopy. It was a massive tangle of tall trees. I stayed at my 20mm post. Finally I became bored with just sitting, waiting for something to happen. Then I felt the urgent need to piss. I did not know the procedure for this. It wasn't like *I'm on a road trip and there is a rest stop 2 miles up the road*. The 20mm turret was like a thick steel soup can with an open top, so I decided to climb up and out of this sweltering metal container and go to the far aft and take a leak.

I was immediately taken with the true beauty of the jungle. The only sounds I heard were the rumbling of the diesel engines of the boats. I unzipped my pants and was just looking around at the scenery, acting pretty much like a moron who was on the jungle ride at Disneyland, not thinking about anything in particular. While taking my leisurely piss I noticed that the color of the river water was a fucking ugly brown. I mean the water color was this horrible brown color with chunks of stuff floating with the river current. Not that I thought the water would be clear blue like a pristine mountain trout stream . . . but shit brown? Then the proverbial light bulb went off! The Brown Water Navy's name *finally hit home*. So that was how the name came about, nice. The large Mekong River where the support ships of the MRF anchored, had the nickname of "The Big Blue." Now it hits home that I am really "in the shit." The clock has started to tick and this game is on for real.

I zipped up my pants and climbed back into the gun turret. I was not in the turret more than a minute when I heard the loud bang of an explosion and the excited voice of the boat captain on the headphones screaming that the convoy was under attack with RPG rounds. The 20mm was cocked and loaded. I peered out through the slit in the turret and I saw what I believed was a lone VC jumping from one side of a tree stump to the other. I thought to myself that this one VC was the reason why I was there. This guy was the reason I spent so many hours, days and weeks training. This was my target. I did not hesitate, I opened fire and hit the tree stump with a long burst of 20mm fire and the stump explodes into hundreds of broken pieces. As fast as the firefight started it was over. It lasted only minutes. We ceased fire and the convoy continued up the canal. I have no clue if I hit him or not but I did not hesitate to fire, so I know my training paid off as I pulled the trigger on command.

I learned four things in those brief minutes: #1. Aiming the cannon accurately through the small slit of the gun turret was not as challenging as I thought it might be. #2. I was a total dumb fuck for exposing myself on the aft of the boat and felt lucky my head was not blown off by a sniper. #3. That wetting yourself thoroughly, even after you just emptied your bladder, is possible. And #4. That when you are new and green you have *no* sense of the danger that lurks around you every hour of every day. I can only imagine Doug Morton felt the same things I was feeling as he plied these waterways on his boat.

A few weeks after the pissing incident another crewman from another boat was pissing off of his boat in what he thought was a secure area. He took an AK-47 round in the chest, the bullet passed through his body and exited out the other side. The heavy round knocked him on his ass. He was given immediate medical help and medevac'd to a field hospital. He was not heard of again for maybe three weeks. Then he just returned to his boat to continue his tour. I did not know him that well but I was there when he showed off his wound and I guess he was extremely lucky as his lungs did not collapse and he recovered quickly enough to get back to work.

For the next three weeks we came and went on operations with frequent contact with the VC. The crew had settled in to the daily routine of life on the river. For some unknown reason the boat captain had switched up the crew posts and I found myself now part of the three man 40mm cannon crew on the forward end or bow of the boat. I was still too new and green to fret about any changes and I gladly accepted my new duties.

The 40mm cannon is a manually operated gun with the two crewmen seated on the carriage supported by a loader (me) feeding four-round clips into the top of the gun. The crewman in the left-hand seat was the pointer who controlled the gun's elevation by turning a crank. The other crewman was the trainer who controlled the right/left movement of the gun with another crank. The crewman in the left seat wore the radio headset and controlled the foot pedal trigger and took direction from the boat captain, directing the line of fire from the cannon. If run smoothly with no complications the 40mm cannon crew could put out 60 rounds a minute of heavy firepower. If the cannon jammed or there was any other malfunction, then precious seconds could pass before the cannon was re-cocked and ready to fire again.

Towards the very end of my tour the Navy introduced new riverboats into the flotilla that were made from scratch, not converted WWII craft. One of the new boats was a monitor that used a 105mm howitzer on the bow that replaced the 40mm cannon. At first glance this looked very impressive and was extremely high powered compared to the 40mm, but on a good day the crew could only get off one round a minute with the 105mm which turned out to be a problem. If the one round fired was not on target this gave Charlie 59 seconds to fire back at the 105mm with as many RPG's as he could muster. I found out from experience 59 seconds could easily feel like 59 minutes inside that turret. The old 40mm cannon had less of a punch but could put out the 60 rounds in a minute which could be enough rounds to keep Charlie at bay.

What I discovered as time went on, is that the 40mm cannon was tough, hazardous duty. I did not know the composition of or what made up the guts of a 40mm shell, but when the rounds were fired the red hot empty brass casings would eject to the bottom of the cannon, generating even more heat inside the turret. The smell of ammonia was very thick inside the turret as well, sometimes it was tough to get fresh air in my lungs.

I was given the loaders job, the same job as my friend Doug Morton got. I sat straddled on top of the cannon feeding 4 round clips into the top of the gun. Lining the inside of the cannon turret were clips of shells within easy reach and as the shells were fired off I would load the new clips of shells into the cannon. This was a very hot, humid, dangerous job, with no ventilation inside the turret and no ear plugs to muffle the tremendous noise of the cannon.

My first firefight inside the turret went smoothly. In the end though I was totally dehydrated from lack of water and I easily lost 10 pounds from sweating. Knowing that if an RPG busted through that turret I was a dead man also made me a little crazy, but "it is what it is" as they say nowadays, and there was nothing that could be done about the way the system was run. I completed my entire tour inside that cannon turret and I was never assigned a different job on the boat. You might think that one only needed to be inside the turret during firefights but that was not the case. Once the convoy entered the small rivers or canals everybody manned their posts, no matter what their jobs were. So when that time came, the three man 40mm crew would take their positions inside the turret and wait for something to happen. You could run the river for 10 hours with no enemy contact but you still had to be at your post.

The inside of the turret was smelly, muggy and hot as hell. Sitting there for long stretches of time became almost unbearable. At the same time you had to be ready to unload the cannon if contact was made with the VC. I kept the small turret hatch open for some ventilation, but as soon as the first rockets struck I would slam the hatch door shut and go to work.

The favorite and most deadly weapon the gooks used against the boats was the shoulder fired RPG7 or B40 rocket that could easily penetrate the ¼" steel of the turrets. In some cases the RPG exited the opposite side of the turret, killing any soul who was in its path. If death himself did not knock on your door you would probably would lose and arm or a leg from the high powered shrapnel the rocket produced upon impact and explosion. This was the death that Doug and I were facing every day on those ugly brown rivers.

After only a month or so of arriving in-country I had become a true combat veteran, having engaged in many firefights. Our crew had handled the situations well, sustaining no injuries or deaths. I had a daily routine for hygiene and meals, still I noticed that I had lost some weight in my first month. This was not a concern, as I felt good and I was still gung-ho for the mission.

I cannot explain fully what it feels like to be in a firefight, other than to say it is extremely noisy but not chaotic in the sense of the crew's work. We worked well together and everybody knew their jobs. When a firefight broke out every man on the boat knew what to do towards the survival of the boat and our own lives.

I had no sense of time inside the turret, the only thing I was vigilant about was that we needed to generate as much firepower as the cannon would allow us to. The more fire we threw at the gooks, the less opportunity they had to fire back at us. It was all about time management and pure luck.

My experience in combat was different than many that served in Vietnam because I was cooped up in a gun turret and never saw the targets we were firing at. My concern was to keep the cannon in operation during the firefight and keep pumping the rounds out as fast as possible. The majority of the firefights I was engaged in were close range, savage battles with loss of life. Perhaps I had a different spin on things because I was unable to see what was going on around us. The cannon turret was a *huge* rocket target. It was never far from my mind that one of those bastards could bust through the turret at any time and change my life forever. I think the attitude of the cannon crew was that the best course of action was to be as offensive as possible, to keep the return fire away from us, lay as much shit down in their direction as we could, so they could not stand up and take aim at the cannon. So, even though I knew that all hell had broken loose on the other side of the turret, my only concern was the three of us on the inside and to keep the shells pumping out at maximum rate.

If I were a ground soldier I could hunker down in the brush for cover or move my position to avoid the fire. The MRF boats were sitting in the middle of a small canal with nowhere to hide, wide open to rocket fire from both sides of the canal. There was no place to hunker down and no place to run. Basically that was it, if you did not have the fire power to return at the enemy, then you could turn off the lights, the party was over.

I knew from the boat captain that our cannon crew did devastating work on the targets that we were directed to fire at. I know that we caused death among the VC. After every firefight the captain would debrief the crew on the operation and told us the cannon crew was always was on target. We always did what we were asked to do.

The country of South Vietnam was divided into 4 military zones from I Corps in the far north by the DMZ to IV corps in the Mekong Delta in the south. The MRF only operated in the rivers and canals of IV Corps but in late February of 1968, RAD 11 was informed that we would be transported by naval ships north to I Corps near the DMZ in support of Task Force Clearwater. We were to provide fire power and river security for the 3rd Marine division operating on the Cua Viet and Perfume rivers in the Quang Tri Province in the far northern part of South Vietnam. A total of 14 riverboats of River Assault Division 11, including us, were transported up the coast line by massive Navy LSD's. These were warships with a well deck that supported amphibious operations like us. After a 5 or 6 day transport we found ourselves approximately 90 miles north of Da Nang and very close to the DMZ . . . in a world totally opposite from the Mekong Delta in the south.

CHAPTER 8

TASK FORCE CLEARWATER

Our destination was Naval Support Activity (NSA) Cua Viet at the mouth of the Cua Viet River. This was a supply base dug out of the white sand beaches which lined the river banks. The NSA was the furthest north of the Navy's bases in Vietnam, Cua Viet was under mortar, rocket, and ground attack by the North Vietnamese Army for the majority of our time there. Because of its location on the Cua Viet River that skirted the boundary of the Demilitarized Zone (DMZ), the base was uniquely situated to provide fuel, ammunition, administration, supplies, and construction materials to Marine and Army combat forces. We were off-loaded by the LSD's two miles off-shore. To dock at the NSA we had to make a treacherous ocean journey that was made more difficult by shifting sand bars at the mouth of the Cua Viet River. I wasn't quite sure that C-112-1 was seaworthy, but she was and we docked without any problems.

NSA provided logistical support to American and allied units operating around the DMZ area and supplied Dong Ha upriver. Our job description was to provide daily firepower and river security from the NSA up the river to a 3rd Marine Division outpost in Dong Ha. We were told that this would be a short mission, possibly 6 to 8 weeks and then back to the Mekong Delta.

I Corps was a total opposite from the delta, with wide open rice paddies lining the river and green mountains in the distance. There were no clinging jungles to maneuver through. However there were many massive rain storms as well as other more immediate dangers. One other very major point. In the Delta the VC were referred to as Charlie. I soon learned that up here near the DMZ the enemy you encountered would be the North Vietnamese Army regulars (NVA) right out of Hanoi. I mean fully uniformed, battle hardened troops, with the respectful nickname of *Mr. Charles*. The average Viet Cong in the Delta was a farmer by day and fighter by night, recruited by certain factions controlled by the North Vietnamese. The VC had AK-47 rifles and of course RPG's. They normally wore no type of uniform to distinguish them as soldiers, they were tough son of bitches who knew how to fight and they were very well disciplined. Mr. Charles wore uniforms like regular soldiers. The NVA also deployed heavy artillery weapons north of the DMZ which had a long range. The NSA at Cua Viet was a favorite target both day and night. This is where I first heard the word "incoming!" when NVA 152mm rounds rained in from the north all around us.

The DMZ was a no man's land which separated the North from the South and was mostly, from what I was told, controlled by and large by the NVA. This is the area in which the NVA set up their big guns to fire south in the direction of I Corps.

On the surface this appeared to be a fairly safe mission, as the Cua Viet was a wide river with no jungle on its banks to obscure the view. We were not ferrying combat troops, just patrolling the river, checking the local river craft for contraband and providing security to supply boats heading to Dong Ha.

The first few nights our convoy of boats were tied up together in a line at the dock and we spent those nights onboard, until we learned that we could sleep in the hooches provided on the base. There was also a good size chow hall, so we had access to hot meals again. The first five nights after arriving there was heavy incoming and a few rounds landed close to the boats. It was determined that in the future all of the boats had to drop anchor in the river and spread out so as not to make too big of a target for the NVA gunners. How did the NVA know where we were? It was soon discovered that the local fishing boats that worked the river near the base were actually spotters for the NVA heavy guns! They would relay the positions of our boats and the supply ships to the gunners north of the DMZ, a distance of 7 or 8 miles. It didn't take long to set a perimeter in the river for these fishing boats and this seemed to help in the weeks to follow in regards to the incoming landing close to the supply ships.

The NSA base was literally carved out of the white sand beaches. The 3rd Marine Division made the base into an armed fortress. They placed 105mm Howitzer big-gun artillery in big pits dug deep into the sand with only the tip of the barrel sticking out of the sand. Then they placed wooden boardwalks all over the complex to make it easier to run or walk over the sand. Bunkers were strategically placed around sleeping quarters for easy access during incoming fire, it was like a comfy home away from home.

The first time I decided to sleep onshore there was incoming at

2:00 AM in the morning and it was a rude awakening. I heard someone scream "Incoming!" and I could hear the artillery shells whistling overhead as they passed very close to the hooch I was sleeping in. I made a mad dash to one of the many sandbag bunkers on the base. The first time I sprinted across the boardwalks towards a bunker my boot got caught in a wooden slat and I stumbled and fell face first into the sand. When I reached the bunker I entered at full speed and slammed my chest into a wooden support beam and it felt like someone shot me in the chest! Being new to the base I didn't know that when you entered a bunker, you made a hard right and then another hard left to get inside, this way if a shell explodes outside the entrance no shrapnel could penetrate the interior of the bunker. The next time I did it correctly. One night the bunker directly next to the one I was in took a direct hit and the explosion was so loud I thought my bunker took the hit! Fortunately there were no serious injuries reported. I soon realized that this duty near the DMZ was just as dangerous as the Mekong Delta. I also realized that there was no safe place to hide, that I could die just as easily there as any place else.

Even though I never saw one, the rumor was that the NVA had tanks not far from this base and that they also had access to Russian MIG fighter jets but I think this was more hype than fact.

The down side of spending time at this base was that officers of the different branches were also there with us. They, unlike us sailors and river rats, demanded and expected their troops to abide to all military codes of conduct. Conduct like: clean and complete uniforms, regulation haircuts, and all the rest of the by-the-book-stuff. Meanwhile I myself, and the others from the boats, were walking around with half laced boots, shaggy hair and facial hair of all descriptions, which all seemed perfectly normal to us.

One of my fellow crewmen was an Italian guy who had thick, black hair stubble on his face. If he did not shave daily he could grow a full beard or mustache in 7 days. To break the boredom he would always sport a new facial hair style monthly. This particular month he had one side of his face clean shaven and the other side of his face was a well-manicured beard and mustache which I rather liked. This style did not bother the boat captain or any other member of the crew. One night he and I decided to go to the base chow hall for dinner and it did not go so well. We stood in line with my favorite guys, the marines, and suddenly

51

a Marine officer walks by and all of the marines in line snap to attention as he walks by . . . except the two of us river rats. Not only is my buddy's beard unusual, but our shirts are not tucked in and our boots are not laced up. The officer passes us and notices my buddy's half-beard and the officer comes unglued. He gets into my buddy's face and demands to know who he is, what branch of the service does he belong to? My buddy is from the south and in a low, southern drawl he tells the officer that we are in the Navy. "What Navy?" the officer demands. "The United States Navy, Sir." he replies, the officer is beside himself with rage. The Marine officer storms off. We did not give it another thought and proceeded to eat dinner.

The other commodity that we possessed but which seemed to have escaped the grasp of the other troops, was that we had plenty of hard liquor onboard, which we had been able to collect when we were in the Delta. The sampans of the locals always had plenty of booze to barter with. One case of C-rations for a bottle of hard liquor was common, and this bartering was done in the open with no fear. This was because it turned out that the boat captain loved his hard stuff.

Sadly not many more nights were spent ashore, as the Marine officer who had yelled at us had filed a complaint with the commanders of the MRF. So we were pretty much barred from using the base facilities. Besides there was too much NVA incoming on the base. It was way safer to stay on the boats. The word was soon put out that all river rats that came ashore were to be in proper uniform and clean shaven, which didn't set well with me, I think my exact words were, "Fuck 'em."

The daily routine was that as early as sunrise and sometime into late morning the convoy would start up river towards Dong Ha. We staggered the starting times, as well as the number in the convoy, so as not to establish a pattern. We would approach the locals in their small fishing boats and sampans to check their cargo and to verify that they were actually fishing or transporting goods. Occasionally body parts were spotted floating in the river and we needed to pull them out and bag and tag them and deliver the parts for recording. I considered this safe duty because you could see for long distances on both sides of the river. The distance to the river banks was too far for an RPG.

We even tried the "winning of hearts and minds" technique by stopping in a few small villages and passing out C-rats to the kids and their families. The other major job was to hunt for and try to disarm any floating water mines that the NVA would put out in the dead of night. These mines were very deadly and could cripple or even sink a mid-size boat, including a boat like ours. The NVA had units of highly trained swimmers and divers whose only job was to place lethal mines in the waterways. We were trained on how to spot the mines prior to running over one. So a major job for the convoy was to hunt for and try to disarm any floating water mines that the NVA would put out in the dead of night. To help detect water mines prior to running over one, the Navy came up with an ingenious idea. They converted an old ATC into a minesweeper and devised a system of chains and hooks on the front ramp of the boat. When the boat was in the river the crew would lower the boat ramp dropping this devise into the water in front of the boat. The idea was that the chains and hooks would detonate any mine in the water prior to the boat hitting the mine. The idea worked, many water mines were exploded in this manner and sometimes this minesweeper would lead the convoy up river paving the way. Our converted ATC boats were able to get rid of a lot of these mines, but not all of them.

There was always plenty of activity around the river, helicopters always flying overhead, tanks and tracked vehicles of all descriptions rumbling around off in the distance, sounds of explosions near and far, fighter jets always above going in every direction as well as attack bombers you could hear but not see with the naked eye.

One night late, as we lay anchored in the river, the boat suddenly started to shake, like an earthquake shake, and I hear this tremendous thundering sound that built in intensity as the seconds ticked by. The boat shook for maybe 90 seconds and I could see flashes in the night just north of the river. We all knew it was something big and we were told the next day that we were as close as you wanted to get to a B52 bomb drop that had happened in the direction of the night flashes we had seen. How anybody could have survived in the path of that barrage was unknown to me. I do not know how far away we were from the bomb's target but it was enough to shake the heavy armored boat in open river water miles from the target area.

You would never know when the NVA were going to throw shells in at NSA. It was a very critical supply base that stored everything from large quantities of fuel, ammunition, bombs and everything else a modern army needed to function. There was a boat repair station as well as a dock where good size Navy ships were always offloading all types of military vehicles and equipment. No wonder NSA was a big target for the NVA.

It was in the afternoon and we were anchored in our spot in the river when I heard incoming whizzing overhead and two rounds landed just feet away from us in the water, I dived for cover and split the palm of my right hand open on a piece of bar armor as I hit the deck. It bled like no tomorrow as I lay with my hands over my head for protection. The captain got out the first aid kit and put a field dressing over my hand, when we heard an extremely loud explosion. I looked to shore and I see a ball of fire coming from the massive ammo dump approx. 600 yards away from us. The NVA gunners were "walking" their shells from the river towards the ammo dump and they scored a direct hit in the middle of the dump. More explosions went off and the captain ordered us to pull anchor and head towards the ammo dump to see if we could give any assistance. Another crewman and myself ran to the bow of the boat just in front of the 40mm turret to get a better look to see if we could find a safe spot to pull up to offer any help. I could see men scrambling around trying to flee the explosions. I thought that if any of them fled into the river we could pick them up. Maybe a 150-200 hundred yards out I saw a tremendous orange flash and a millisecond later I felt the concussion of the blast slam into my chest. It pushed me back about 6 feet into the 40mm turret. I hit the turret and fell to the deck of the boat. My ears were ringing loudly and I felt punch drunk as I got to my feet. I saw my buddy lying next to me. He was hit by the same concussion. I looked at him and he looked like I felt, dazed and confused. We both staggered to the back of the boat. Now the captain realized that the boat crew was in big danger. He gave orders to the coxswain to turn the boat around and head back to the middle of the river. It seems a 1000 pound bomb exploded in the ammo dump fire and the concussion from the explosion pushed us back like we were nothing. I do know men were killed and injured in the attack. The fire from the ammo dump burned for a couple of days. It took some time for my head to finally clear out the cobwebs.

As my tour continued the ringing in my ears became louder and more annoying. I think that the combination of no ear plugs inside the cannon turret, coupled with that bomb blast that knocked me on my ass, had caused some damage to my hearing. I wrote this off as a minor inconvenience compared to the guys who had died or had lost an arm or a leg. It was all just part of that hazardous duty.

The cut on my right hand was deep and it took some time for the bleeding to stop. The boat captain asked me if I wanted to go see a Navy corpsman to get it looked at. I told him I thought I was okay and that I didn't need any stitches. I thought to myself that if I went to see a Navy corpsman for the gash he would think that I was a pussy, whining over a cut on my hand. These guys saw wounds a million times worse than this cut. So I just wore the field bandage to keep the cut covered and hoped I wouldn't get an infection. Later that day the boat captain told me that I needed to get the paper work started for a Purple Heart medal and I got really confused. I didn't think that a cut on the hand justified a Purple Heart, but the captain argued that in a combat zone a wound was a wound. He asked me if I planned on making the Navy a career? Because if I did then a Purple Heart would look mighty good on my service record and be very helpful for future promotions.

My thinking was this, if I had to ask for or request a purple heart I wasn't interested. If receiving this medal was for the purpose of building up my service record to make me look good, then I *really* wasn't interested. It did make me realize that even in the middle of a war there were people who were scheming to make things better for themselves in the future. I'm no saint, but I saw no advantage for me in asking for the Purple Heart, so I declined. Actually I told the boat captain to "fuck off" and put the issue to rest, which he did.

On March 14th the good fortune of the MRF in I Corps came to an end when T-112-7 boat hit a water mine and killed the 6 crew onboard. The high intensity explosion flipped the boat in the air and onto its back and sank it with only part of the broken hull showing above the water. It was very late in the afternoon with a high tide. After determining there were no survivors the decision was made to recover the bodies early the next morning, it was simply too dangerous for the divers to dive in the dark with the swift river currents.

The next day at sunrise we made the trip upriver along with a few other boats to the location of the doomed ATC. We secured that portion of the river so the divers could do their work. In short time a Navy corpsman boarded our boat and we moved forward and positioned ourselves next to the sunken boat to allow the divers to bring up the bodies and put them on the bow of the boat. That way the corpsman could examine them. Our crew was told to stay on the aft of the boat as not to interfere with this task. Still, I could clearly see the severely wounded, water-bloated bodies of these sailors as they were brought onboard. Each one was examined and put into a body bag. The mood among our crew was extremely sorrowful. We knew that these guys were part of the group from our training class. Now here they lay in body bags on the bow of our boat, their families soon to be notified about their deaths. The divers reported that overnight the NVA had sent their own divers down and stripped the ATC clean of all ammo, weapons and personal belongings, anything of value on that boat was gone. So we couldn't dive at night, but the NVA could, dismantling a boat in the dark waters of a rapidly flowing river. These NVA were fucking tough customers.

Soon all of the doomed crew of the ATC was onboard and we headed up river to Dong Ha to off-load the bodies. I'm not sure if I volunteered or was ordered, but when we arrived at Dong Ha I assisted in off-loading the body bags to shore. The river was at low tide, when we reached the dock to off-load the body bags, there was a 10 foot distance up from the deck of the boat to the dock. There were a group of marines reaching down to retrieve the body bags from us and one by one we lifted the bags over our heads up to the marines above. When I went to lift one of the body bags the zipper on my end of the bag was not 100% closed and as I hoisted the bag over my head all of the fluid in the bag came rushing out and saturated my body, soaking my head, shirt and pants. At first I was disgusted but quickly realized it was not me in the bag and I was grateful I was alive and in one piece. The pre-Vietnam me in this same situation would have freaked out and probably would have puked my guts out and started to cry, dropped the bag on the deck and yelled out some obscenity. Sadly I was no longer a normal 19 year old kid but rather a battle hardened soul who was saddened by this event but not willing to get emotional about it. I was one who had grown to accept this life in Vietnam and everything that went with it. Still, it was very surreal in every aspect. The war had matured me in an abnormal way, I could now accept the violence of war and the death of people I knew and show no outside emotion. I did not cry or become violent when I witnessed scenes like that. I had instead began the art of burying my emotions deep inside of me. I knew there would be more violence to come, more tragic scenes to witness and perhaps I too would be part of a dramatic and violent end. So I said nothing and continued on with the task at hand. This had been a heart breaking morning. The tough part was the twisted remains of the ATC were never removed, so every day forward we passed the wreck on our daily patrols.

In the 3rd week of April we headed up river for another daily patrol. We were the first patrol boats on the river that day. Somewhere before Don Ha we rounded a bend on the river and suddenly there was a burst of chatter on the convoy's radio. Somebody had spotted something. So I looked ahead to see what was going on. The sun had just risen and I couldn't believe what I saw! An enormous group of fully uniformed NVA troops in the process of crossing the Cua Viet River in small sampan craft. Perhaps a couple hundred NVA troops were crossing the river! The convoy quickly positioned for attack. This would be the first time since arriving in I Corps that my 40mm would be used in action and I was extremely anxious to start firing.

It appeared that maybe 10% or so of the NVA had already crossed the river and the remaining were waiting their turn to cross. I personally thought that once we began firing there was little chance of them returning fire as they all turned and started to run for cover. The convoy began firing and moving closer to the river bank to get within a closer range of the NVA. On the side of the river they were crossing from there was a tree line perhaps a mile back. This was the direction towards which they were fleeing. We had caught them by surprise and in the open. A few of the boats were directing their fire towards the NVA who had already crossed over, but they were closer to cover and appeared to have made it quickly to safety. Air support was called in as the convoy put out all the fire power we had.

I had never been in a one sided firefight before and we threw as much fire at them as possible. Soon the NVA were out of our reach. At that same time the first fighter jets from the Da Nang area and a Navy carrier off the coast, arrived on scene. The river was shut down in both directions and we were ordered to stay put, patrol and provide security. At this point we were out of the fight and I pull out my 8mm movie camera and shot film of the fighter jets dropping their bombs on the NVA. As the Navy jets began their bombing sorties, the boat pulled back to what was thought a safe distance to avoid shrapnel flying our way from about a 1/4 mile away. I stood behind the 40mm turret for protection and balanced the movie camera on top of the turret aiming the camera on the bombs as they fell to earth. When the first bomb exploded it shook the boat and I tucked my head down to protect myself from flying metal and debris. The explosions shook the entire craft in open river water from over a 1/4 mile away, these had to be 1000 pound bombs. I was able to shoot for 5 or 6 minutes when the boat captain finally realized we were too close to the action. He ordered the lumbering C-112-1 at full speed to a safer distance across the river. From what I could see as the bombardment continued most of the NVA had made it to the tree line, but I believe there were many that perished in the open fields. The bombing of the tree line lasted well over an hour and it seemed impossible that anybody could have survived that pounding. Once again I would be proven wrong.

By late morning the 3rd Marine Division was staging hundreds of troops in the open fields, supported by tanks and amphibious vehicles. It was clear the marines were going to make an assault on the tree line, the marines had information there were hundreds more NVA hunkering down in there. The fighter jets were still in the area but flying much higher than when bombing. Transport helicopters "jolly green giants," were bringing in more marines and more support helicopters were everywhere. The standard field radio was called a PRC or "Prick" radio. I pulled one out to see if I could receive any of the channels the marines were using. This day would be one of the saddest days for me in my Vietnam tour. I wasn't even involved in the fight at this point, I was strictly an observer and it was about to become brutal.

The marines advanced towards the tree line. It was hard to make out what exactly what was going on with the naked eye but from the distance I began to hear lots of weapons and support fire from helicopters and tanks. The river was secure and we just sat around waiting to see how this would play out. There was not a lot for us to do. I kept searching the channels and suddenly the PRC crackled with life. Units were screaming out for help and directing artillery fire near their positions. It was crystal clear that the marines had made contact with the NVA and the battle was brutal and bloody.

There was one discussion about how to get the wounded out of the area and the decision made was that the fire was so heavy from the NVA the choppers could not safely evacuate the wounded. I heard something about using small craft or boats but the chatter was very hectic and confusing and I was lost on what they decided to do. I knew from personal experience that firefights are extremely loud and they came over the PRC in the same way.

I could see nothing with the naked eye and relied on the radio for any information about the fight in and beyond the tree line. This fight went on for hours. Around 2:00 or 3:00 in the afternoon small 14 foot "Boston Whaler boats" began filing past our boat heading into a small tributary of the river. To me this could only mean one thing; the boats were going in to retrieve the wounded and the dead. Within the next hour the boats were coming out and passing directly beneath me. I saw the body bags piled up on each boat with a tag on the end of each bag. I wanted to film what I saw but I did not have the courage to pick up the camera and film. Boat after boat passed by filled with body bags; it was an incredibly sad sight to see and I had no thoughts running through my head, I was numbed by what I witnessed.

This action lasted into early evening, when we were finally released to return to our mooring spot. I can't tell you what the name of the operations was. I can't tell you the exact date it took place. I cannot tell you how many marines were KIA that day, or how many wounded were carted off. What I can tell you is that it was something I will never forget. Our tour in I Corps had become pretty stressful. Six of our guys killed by a mine in March and we still had some time left here near the DMZ and you never knew what tomorrow would bring.

The difference between I Corps and IV Corps was we did not have the weekly firefights and I rarely was in the cannon turret during our time near the DMZ. The thing we did have was the constant rain of incoming artillery from the NVA which were deadly accurate. If you could hear the whistling of the incoming rounds then you were in immediate danger, as this was the signal that the incoming was at a low altitude and in some cases just feet above your head. I cannot accurately describe the whistling sound the incoming shells make other than maybe the noise you hear from a high pitched jet engine, the difference would be that the shells are traveling at such a high rate of speed that the whistling comes and goes in a matter of seconds, followed by a tremendous explosion. The two rounds that landed near the boat the day of the dump explosion were the closest I experienced and they hit about 10 feet in the water from the boat. If they had made contact with our boat the explosion would have sunk us and surely caused casualties among our crew. When I had heard the whistling noise I had only micro seconds to take cover and I was fortunate that I only ripped open the palm of my hand.

Around the 2nd or 3rd week of May we were told we were heading back to the Delta. I was actually excited about leaving I Corps and heading back to the Delta. For some odd reason I felt more secure there than at the NSA. Again there was no safe haven anywhere we operated, so it was a crap shoot no matter where we were.

It was around this time that I learned of the death of my friend Doug Morton. Doug was hit by a B-40 rocket during a fire fight. The round penetrated the 1/4 inch armor plating of his gun turret and hit him in the side of the head, which literally blew his head off. The rocket exploded when it hit him and it was all over. The impact was so powerful and hard that part of the rocket kept going right through the other side of the turret. It was such a mess that a small hand scraper was used to scrape away bits and pieces of brain and skull from the inside of the cannon turret. Doug Morton died on April 4th, 1968. I can't tell you how much I hated that news. There are no words to describe how sad I was about his death. In sailor's terms it was like "Fuck me! How many more people do I know and care about who will perish in this conflict?" I wondered too if our crew could make it to the end untouched. I was also more than aware that Doug and I had the very same job. I wondered if he, like me, had questioned if and when an RPG was going to rip through his gun turret? Did he have the same fears as I did during a firefight? He must have. War is a stressful occupation at best and I thought that all us river rats had a very high probability of having our asses whipped permanently before this is all over. Everyone I knew felt the same way. I was sure Doug Morton had the same feelings. It was his number that came up. Not mine. And that screwed with my head. The death of Doug Morton was a game changer for me. That was the point in my tour that I went from gung-ho for the mission to "I don't give a shit" about the war. My only goal going forward from that point was purely selfish, do my job and get the fuck off of the dark side of the moon.

I was 4 months into my 12 month tour and I had doubts about the chances of any victory in that war. I was concerned that Doug Morton may have given his life for a lost cause. He had been my friend from back home. His mother would be devastated. Hell mine would be to, since she had worked with Mrs. Morton. That was one thing, the

60

other was the very creepy feeling of being stuck in the same job, on a similar boat in the same damned Brown Water Navy facing exactly what Doug had faced. So now I was really concerned for the welfare of myself and my crew.

COMMANDER
UNITED STATES NAVAL FORCES
VIETNAM

The Secretary of the Navy takes pleasure in presenting the Navy Achievement Medal to

CHARLES GEORGE NESBITT
SEAMAN
UNITED STATES NAVY

for service as set forth in the following

CITATION

"For professional achievement while serving with United States Forces engaged in riverine assault operations against the Viet Cong communist aggressors in the republic of Vietnam. During the period February 1968 to December 1968, Seaman NESBITT served as forty millimeter cannon trainer on board Command and Communications Boat 112-1, a unit of River Assault Squadron ELEVEN engaged in support operations with elements of the Second Brigade, Ninth Infantry Division, United States Army. Seaman NESBITT participated in operations involving numerous combat missions which struck deep into the enemy infested water of the Mekong Delta and inflicted heavy losses to the enemy. During these operations, Command and Communications Boat 112-1 received heavy rocket, recoilless rifle, automatic weapons, and small arms fire in savage, short-range encounters with the enemy. Despite exceedingly long operational periods, he unfailingly met the requirements of the combat situation with enthusiasm and determination. His efforts were instrumental in keeping his boat in a combat operational status and fighting it to its full capability, which significantly contributed to the combat effectiveness of Command and Communications Boat 112-1. Seaman NESBITT's superior performance of duty, sense of responsibility, and courage under fire were in keeping with the highest traditions of the United States Naval Service."

Seaman NESBITT is authorized to wear the Combat "V".

For the Secretary of the Navy

E. R. ZUMWALT, Jr.
Vice Admiral, U. S. Navy
Commander U. S. Naval Forces, Vietnam

Citation for the Navy Achievement Medal, 1969
Awarded to Charlie Nesbitt

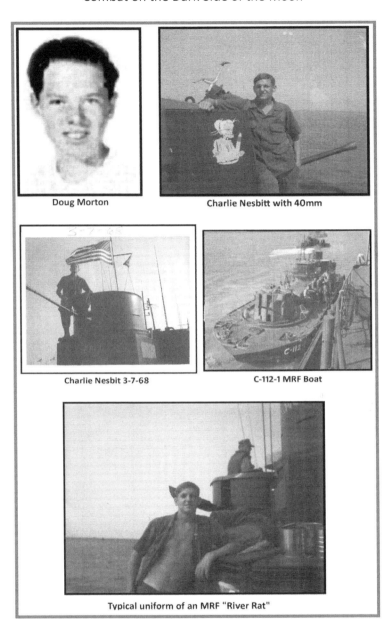

Doug Morton

Charlie Nesbitt with 40mm

Charlie Nesbit 3-7-68

C-112-1 MRF Boat

Typical uniform of an MRF "River Rat"

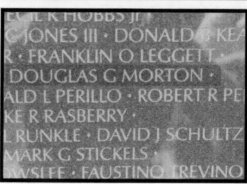

Doug's name on the Vietnam War Memorial Wall

Doug Morton's headstone

We never wore our patches but we had some

My Vietnam Service medal

My Vietnam Service Medal Certificate

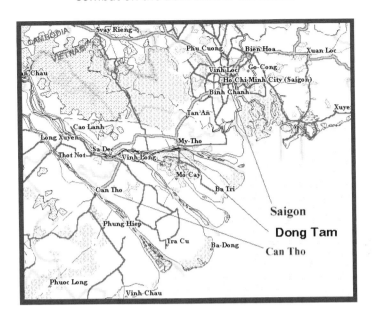

Chapter 9

DELTA BOUND

We were transported back to Dong Tam in the same fashion as our trip up there. We were given a few days off before going back to the routine of daily operations. I just wanted to get drunk and/or finally smoke opium for the first time. Since hearing about Doug's death I had lost my will to stay positive and gung ho. I needed something to help me cope with daily life on the boats.

Since day one of arriving at Dong Tam I had heard about the smoking of opium by American troops in the Delta. The dope was easy to obtain, as the VC used opium as a normal part of their day, it was part of their culture. After any firefight the Army would do a sweep of the area and if they came across any dead VC they searched the bodies for any information that might be helpful. I was told that opium was frequently found on the bodies, wrapped in black silk cloth. The opium was taken and used by some of the troops and they often shared it with the crews of the riverboats. Prior to the Navy I had never so much as smoked a cigarette, let alone dope, but in the Delta opium was always available if I wanted it.

It came down to age, if you were over the age of maybe 25 or so you drank hard liquor, under the age of 25 you smoked opium. The longer you were in-country the more susceptible you were to trying something to get through the hardships of daily life. Since joining the Navy I had already taken up the habit of smoking and in Vietnam the cigarettes were free. They were included in every case of combat rations. You even had your choice of menthol or regulars. I was smoking 2 to 3 packs of cigarettes a day and it never crossed my mind that they were addictive or bad for your health, hell I might have my head blown off just like Doug tomorrow, so why worry about a few cigarettes?

The story goes that the VC commanders provided opium to their troops for a couple of reasons; one is that it was less expensive to produce opium than rice; it appeared that when you used opium on a regular basis the opium suppressed your desire for food so you'd eat less each day, which would cut down the daily rice rations needed to feed an army. The second reason was that opium can make you feel

66

superhuman, the dope skews up your whole being and you will do more crazy things and take more chances when you smoke opium. You were not a crybaby when you were high on this shit. I was told once you smoked opium you did not want to quit, that you felt more comfortable in your "own skin" and the burden of combat was eased. I was intrigued and for a while it worked.

So as the summer of 1968 progressed and I turned 20 years old, I was trying to find a way to mentally escape from this madness I found myself in. Hard liquor was not my usual thing, so one night a group of us were playing poker and some opium was passed around and I took a hit, then another and another. To say I took a trip on opium would be an understatement. I did not know what to expect. I had no idea how fantastic the opium would make me feel or what a mind blower the stuff could be. By the end of the night I had to lie down because my head was no longer attached to my body. I mean I was lying flat on my back and I could not feel my head with my hands, I looked to the left of me and I could see my head a few feet away rolling back and forth, I could see my hands covering my rolling head. I didn't freak out but I couldn't figure out what to do next so I fell asleep thinking that maybe my head would be reattached when I woke up. It was. I think the problem was I smoked way too much shit and combined with hard liquor my poor confused mind just could not handle it.

I smoked opium regularly from then on, as this was my escape from what was going on around me. It was not uncommon to smoke dope as we headed up a canal or river on the start of an operation, there were some firefights where I was high inside the cannon turret; but most of the dope smoking or drinking of hard liquor was done at night when we had free time. I do not for a moment suggest that everyone on the riverboats, including our crew, got drunk or smoked dope. Every riverboat crew and captain was different and they coped with the war in their own way. You became extremely close with your own crew and each boat was almost like a small business working independently of each other for the greater cause. Quite frankly I didn't give a crap about other boat crew's ethics or morals, just ours. This was the period in my tour where I was having a moral battle within myself, how I easily justified in my mind using dope and buying whores was A Okay. On one hand I knew that some of my conduct was a free pass to hell but on the other hand I might make it through this fucking mess unscathed and ask God to forgive me later, it was like rolling the dice and hope for the best. So the bottom line is many of the out of this world experiences I had on the dark side of the moon were self-inflicted and of my own actions, they had nothing to do with Vietnam. The mind of a 19 year old kid under heavy stress in a foreign land is a hard thing to control or predict and I did what I thought was the best for me at that time.

The only option for obtaining other types of drugs, blocks of river ice, local girls and liquor was from the civilians in sampans. They would barter anything for a few cases of C-rats, of which we always had plenty onboard. After we allowed a sampan to pull alongside our boat and we had completed a safety check of the sampans contents, we could barter for whatever the locals wanted to sell. Hard liquor was a favorite for some of the crew, while I usually traded for small, river water ice blocks to cool down with. You couldn't use the ice to cool drinking water as the river water was highly polluted and not safe to drink; but it certainly would cool down your neck on the hot, humid days. As far as the liquor, you had to be very cautious that you were trading with un-tampered seals on the bottles, because a favorite trick of the VC was to grind up glass and put it into the liquor bottles for unsuspecting soldiers to drink down. I remember one of the crew who used to shake the bottle and put it in front of a light bulb prior to paying up, to make sure there was nothing unusual floating around in the liquor. There was never a fear of being busted for smoking dope. It was a common practice and the only time our crew refrained from liquor or dope is when Commander Sullivan was onboard during operations.

This guy Commander Sullivan was a strange duck and all Navy. He habitually wore an Australian wool military hat of some sort and he did not fraternize with the crew. I never once had one word with the man and he kept to himself, but he knew his stuff and he was, for the most part, respected by the crew. One thing was for sure though, he was one tough son of a bitch and he did not hesitate to stand up in the middle of a firefight and direct the troops. His vanity though, was totally over the top.

At the tail end of one firefight the wind caught his Aussie hat and it flew into the canal, he screamed at the coxswain, "Turn this fucking tub around!" One of the crew grabbed the long metal pole that we used to fetch body parts and tried to snatch his hat as it floated on the water.

There was still VC activity in the area but that didn't bother Sullivan, he was right there with the crewman trying to snag that hat. The hat was finally retrieved and we got back in line with the convoy. Dereliction of duty because of some stupid hat? Not in Sullivan's mind. The hat was more important than any operation the Navy might have had in mind.

Somewhere near the base at Dong Tam was a small village or town and if the boats were at the base the Navy allowed us to go to the village as long as we were back onboard by sundown. There was a staging area where the men could catch a ride into town and the same on the other end coming back. I had met this rather large, red haired guy from another boat and he told me about this town and the few bars that he had visited while he was there. He assured me it was safe as long as you got out of the village before sunset. So the next time I had a few days off I decided to give it a try.

A few of us from the crew went to the staging area and found Red and another guy. We hitched a ride with the Army to this town. I remember it was a two lane dirt road that cut through farm land and was not too terribly far from the base. We arrived at the center of the town and there were plenty of troops there so I felt okay about it. We went to this bar he liked and the first thing I noticed was there were metal bars on the windows and the front door (to keep out hand grenades I was told). There was a rundown juke box playing old American western songs and maybe 8 or 9 other troops sitting around a table. We sat at the bar and I started to drink beer, lots of beer. Everybody in the place was wearing a sidearm except me; I had this thing about guns on my hip. I just didn't like them. After a few hours we heard this commotion on the narrow street outside the bar. I looked outside to see what was up. There was an American jeep with two MP's facing an ARVN jeep with two QC's (ARVN military police) and there is no room for them to pass each other. They were yelling at each other and it had become a Mexican stand-off, neither was going to move for the other. I found this amusing until I heard gunfire and we all hit the deck! "What the hell!?" somebody yells as the two military cops take pot shots at each other. It ended as quickly as it started and it appeared to end with no harm no foul. This was like drinking in some old west town in Arizona.

After a bit, Red asked the bartender if there was any place close we could get some "boom-boom." He excitedly pointed across the street to this old, three story hotel and yells; "Yes, yes, boom-boom!" He told us to go into the lobby and pay the clerk for anything we wanted. So, after many hours of hard drinking, we hauled ourselves across the street and went inside.

It was a very old, rundown hotel and the clerk spoke okay English. He told us to pay him up front and then go up the stairs to the second floor. "If you find an open door to a room there will be a girl inside." Only Red and me decided to pay, so up the stairs we went to the second floor. The door was opened to the first room I came to. I see a Vietnamese girl my age or younger sitting on the bed and I figured why not? Red continued down the hall as I entered the room and shut the door.

The girl was wearing a simple, thin cloth robe and flashes me a big smile. Carrying a rubber for protection was not part of the uniform and it really never crossed my mind to worry about those things. I went over to the bed and she motioned for me to take down my pants. I complied, lay down on my back and she motioned for me to roll over on my stomach, which I did, and she then proceeded to walk on my back! Now this girl did not weigh more than 80 pounds and this foot massage felt really good, but I wondered if this was what I paid for. No matter, it felt good. She walked slowly from top to bottom and then starts to yell in Vietnamese at her girlfriend in the other room through paper thin walls. It seems Red is getting the same treatment next door and I guess they are just doing some girl talk. After 10 minutes or so she gets down from my back and pulls her robe off and motioned for me to roll on my back, which I did.

She spoke broken English with a lot of hand gestures and told me how she loves Americans and she climbs on top of me. I was starting to sober up and I was ready to get busy, when she points up towards the ceiling and says in her broken English "VC up there boom-boom." I said, "What?" and she repeats, "VC boom-boom like you now up there." I was now totally sober and I ask her if she meant there were VC on the next floor doing boom-boom like me? She nods her head yes. I put my hands on her hips and deposited her on the bed next to me, jumped off and grabbed my pants, struggling to put my boots on, I headed out the door. I opened the door where my buddy was and in a whisper I tell him we have to *get out now, don't ask questions let's just go!* We shuffled down the stairs to the lobby and out the front door. The others we had come with were gone. Laughing, we started on our way back to the staging area to catch a ride back to the base.

It suddenly dawned on me that it was very late in the afternoon and by the time we reached the spot for our ride we both realized that maybe it is too late in the day for a ride back to the base. Sure enough the area was nearly empty of activity. I started to feel sick to my stomach. It wasn't the booze that was making me feel that way, it was the fear. There was absolutely no place to stay in this village for the night, plus we were unarmed. I see one Army sergeant on the road and I rushed over to him to get some information. He told me that sundown was less than a half hour away. He didn't think any more traffic was heading our way that night, but you never knew. Just then an empty troop transport arrived and he agreed to take us. There was a catch though, he was only going to the halfway mark on the road where there was a small bridge that crossed over a small river. He told me there was a platoon of 9th Infantry troops at the bridge and he would be happy to drop us off there. We looked at each other and decided to roll the dice and go with the transport, hoping that maybe we could find a way back from the bridge to the base. It was just turning dark when we reached the bridge. At least we were out of that crazy town. We jumped out and walked over to the army guys near the bridge. We explained our situation to them and we were told that they would be at this location for another 30 minutes and then they were heading out for a night patrol. What we wanted to do after they left on patrol was up to us.

I prayed very few times while I was in-country but I'm sure this was one of the times I prayed and prayed hard. I was very nervous and it was nearly dark. The platoon was getting ready to depart the bridge when we spotted headlights coming our way. A jeep stopped at the bridge. One of the army guys talked to the driver of the jeep while pointing at us. I ran over to the jeep, probably still praying, and asked the driver if he was heading towards the base. He nodded yes and told us to jump in and hold on. Driving out there solo at night was most certainly suicide and he gunned the jeep and we headed towards the base.

The driver said nothing and was driving as fast as he could in the pitch black night. I'm thinking to myself that death is just around the corner. It was only a matter of time before green tracer fire would be zeroed in on us! All three of us were going to die in a barrage of AK47 fire; or an RPG was going to nail the side of the jeep!

Alas my nightmare scenario didn't happen. The base appeared before our eyes and we cruised in unharmed. We were safe! It is funny how the brain reacts to fear one moment then switches to comedy and pure relief the next. As we were speeding down the road in total blackness I was thinking about an RPG busting through the jeep and throwing us off of the road killing the 3 of us and I wondered what the US Navy would have told my mom & dad about my death. Would it have been that I died while cutting a path through a division of VC desperately trying to reach my buddies on the other side who were in grave danger? Or maybe "We regret to inform you that your son died while speeding away from a whore house while trying to make curfew at the base." I actually laughed at my own sick sense of humor but regardless I was happy to be back at the base unharmed.

Instead of thanking God and my good luck, I told myself this was no big deal and I knew we would make it back okay with no problem. You would think that this would be the last time I would foolishly go back to that village. You'd think that I had learned a valuable lesson about liquor, fucking the locals in a nest of VC and driving in the middle of the night in Charlie's territory unarmed. If that is what you thought that you would have been wrong, a couple times wrong.

Chapter 10

CLUSTER FUCK

"When numerous things go wrong in the same time frame" that is the definition of a "cluster fuck." You think to yourself what else could possibly go wrong and it gets even worse, well that is a cluster fuck. I'm not sure if this was a military term or not but I had never heard of it until Vietnam. Some operations went very smoothly and some were full-blown cluster fucks. The boat breaks down the same time the cannon malfunctions. Meanwhile the gooks are throwing everything at you but the kitchen sink. The boat captain is in a foul mood because he drinks too much. We are sent on an operation with too few boats and troops. We are overwhelmed because somebody in intelligence got it wrong, this is a cluster fuck.

There were a lot of times I just didn't get it. Why were we in this spot when we got our asses whipped here just last month? What was the command thinking sending us down the same old beaten track time and time again? This was a cluster fuck.

It was the middle of August that we approached an area called the "Crossroads" on the Ben Tre Canal where two weeks prior the convoy was involved in a large firefight causing, again, loss of life both for the Navy and the Army. When I looked out the turret hatch and saw the two rivers crossing I mumbled my favorite words, "What the fuck" I couldn't believe we were back in the same spot again, going around in circles. This was a cluster fuck.

Fighter jets released their pay load 500 yards short and take out 15 friendlies. Meanwhile the boats were going in circles because nobody really knew where the fuck Charlie was. We fired away at nothing because this is what we did for no reason. This was a cluster fuck.

Under orders from Command we would be enter small canals with sharp switchback turns that we all knew spelled *ambush*, because the convoy was too long and spread out. When you made these sharp turns in the canals it puts half of the boats in the middle of the turn, making the boats vulnerable to rocket attacks from both sides of the river. If a boat broke down from enemy fire it could clog the canal lane, backing up the other boats and causing chaos when the gooks opened fire. Some canals were so narrow that the gooks would sit in the overhanging trees and drop grenades on the boats as they passed beneath. Any moron with a brain would not send a convoy of boats into a small twisting canal like this, but it happened all the time.

At one point the casualty rate for both the Navy and Army was so high that the rumor was that the MRF was going to be dismantled, an exercise in failure. The MRF did a lot of great work and killed a lot of the enemy but there comes a point where the military strategy and the logistics of the whole thing no longer makes any sense.

Years after the war I went to see the movie Good Morning Vietnam with Robin Williams shortly after it was released. I really enjoyed it despite a movie critic who panned the film stating that there were too many scenes of soldiers just sitting around doing nothing, playing football, drinking, etc. The truth is the movie was very close to reality, as there was a lot of down time with nothing to do, you are not always on an operation or in a firefight, there were times the operations were many days apart and there was a lot of smoking dope and drinking to fill the void. The old saying went, "In the military it's a lot of hurry up and wait." That turned out to be true for the most part.

Our boat captain was a drunk and he was showing signs of severe mental stress. It all came to a head in a small firefight during a routine operation. The boat had received normal amounts of rocket fire and all of the crew were doing their jobs when it was noticed that the captain was not on the headphones directing fire for our 40mm cannon. We were firing blindly. One of the crew sprinted down to the communication center to find the captain, he was found in the fetal position lying on the floor near the bunks. He was dead drunk and had reached his breaking point. The only memory I have of the rest of the incident was that when we returned to Dong Tam he was escorted off. We never heard a word about him again. Our new captain arrived within days and the crew went on with the war as usual. Strangely nobody on the crew ever talked about or mentioned the incident, it just didn't matter to us, nobody cared.

I had grown very fond of smoking opium. I was smoking 3 or 4 days a week and drinking warm beer during beer call which was a couple of times of month. It was very bizarre about the beer call because that event would take place immediately after the mandatory Non-Denominational Service for the Dead of the previous weeks. Everybody who was not on an operation gathered at this large docking area that was attached to the large support ship in the middle of the river. Combat boots were placed in a row to represent the dead, if the dead were a sailor there would be a white Navy hat sat on the boots, if Army a combat helmet was placed on the boots. Depending on how many weeks of remembrance were represented there might be as many as 40 to 50 pairs of boots on the dock and the memorial service would begin. I hated this part of my tour, I attended many of these memorials and I could hardly get through them, as the Navy chaplain would recite the same verses and perform the same routine each time, which was followed by BEER CALL. Nothing like putting you in the mood for a couple of warm beers than a memorial service to remember the dead, but this is how it was done.

One night after drinking my two beers there was a commotion on the other side of the dock, men were yelling to give a hand and I ran over to see what was up. Somebody fell off the dock into the swift dark currents of the river and was presumed drowned. Very bright onboard ship lights were lit up and a chopper was dispatched to fly over the river to begin a search. The bright lights made everyone nervous because of constant enemy presence, but the bottom line was that this poor soul had lost his life during beer call. The body to my, knowledge, was never found. This person broke the cardinal rule of living on the river, which is to never lace your combat boots to the top eye of the boot; you only laced them up maybe ¼ of the way. If you fell into the river you could kick them off when lightly laced. Fully laced the boots acted like an anchor and took you to the bottom of the river.

As I said before anything immoral or illegal you wanted was available on the river from the locals who bartered for cases of combat rations in exchange for hard liquor, local girls, blocks of river water ice and other forms of dope like black tar heroin. Because of this, our crew was always very cautious when a small sampan approached us offering their wares to trade. After a quick security search you obtained what they had to trade. The normal trade was hard liquor for combat rations, but the occasional girl trade was done and whoever wanted to partake would do so. Most of these girls were either our age or younger. It would be a quick deal and it was over. I did have sex with these girls, but soon thought better of it because I did not use protection. However, dumb ass me had no problem using no protection when I went into the village for girls, but from some idiotic reason I thought it was a bad idea not use protection when the girls came to the boat.

That's how it was for us on the river. The boredom and idle time could go on for days and this is when your mind begins to justify that you could do stupid things you would not normally do if you were with, let's say, your family. We would usually play poker at night and pass around the dope or a bottle of hard liquor. Nobody I remember ever talked about politics or how the place blew. Rather we laughed a lot at each other and tried to get through another night with humor and stimulants. Some guys stayed to themselves. Still, nearly every person I served with used some kind of stimuli to get through their tours. It was all about mental survival. How could you escape the madness of it all, if only for a few minutes or hours? Dope and liquor were the easiest ways. I suppose some people prayed. I believed in God. Strangely though, I rarely prayed or asked God to help me get through the tour. In reality I turned my back on God and I relied on luck (more like dumb luck), as the days dragged on.

I woke up one early morning on an operation and took my morning piss off the bow of the boat. I had this burning sensation in my penis. I looked down and my urine was a stale yellow color and the burning sensation was nearly unbearable. I thought I knew what the problem was and a few days later I see one of the Army medics and he confirms I have the "clap." I had contracted Gonorrhea and I needed to take penicillin to get rid of the VD. You would think that alarm bells would be sounding in my brain! Yet as with all things Vietnam, it did not signify anything was wrong or unusual for me, I was still alive with two arms and two legs. It took some time for the VD to clear up and I continued my ways sexually with the locals like the VD never happened.

My last clear memory of going to the village for girls was sometime that summer. I felt so comfortable going there that I went alone but still wore no weapon. I went to the same bar as I always visited. I started to drink and have a conversation with a couple of Army guys. Then I noticed this very refined young woman sitting at the bar talking to the bartender. I finally made eye contact and she smiled at me, my signal to move in. She spoke very good English. After some small chit-chat she asked if I wanted to see her "room." I said yes I did want to see her room. She led me through the village to a very small house not too far from the bar. She was very pretty and not too far from my age. I was following her like a small puppy being led to food. We entered this small home and in the front room are a group of people watching a very small screen black & white TV; there is an old man and woman and three or four small children. The girl grabbed my hand and led me to a back room of the house as the old man looked up at me and nodded his head, I smiled back at him. Near the back room of the house was the most peculiar thing, there were four or five bags of rice sitting on the floor and stamped on the bags was something to the effect of "Made in America for the people of South Vietnam." How strange was this to me? I'm in a house surrounded by rice paddies and these people are eating rice from America, this war makes no logical sense to me. But I live for the moment, so we went to her bedroom. She told me that the people in the front room were her family and that they all loved Americans. She said that I might die any day in this war and she wanted me to have a good time today and forget about the war for a few hours. I concur and we began. She was very tender and loving and I felt very comfortable being in her home, so comfortable that I came back the next day for a repeat appearance. What little cash I had was quickly spent, besides the maintenance on the boat was complete and I knew that this was the last time I would be coming to the village as we were scheduled to go on extended operations to areas we had not been to before.

My mind was twisted and confused. I hated the violence, but I did not want to be a KIA, or lose my arms or legs, so I just continued on the path that had gotten me that far. Since joining the military I had lost my virginity, had learned how to pay for sex, smoke multiple packs of cigarettes a day, use profanity as my primary language, smoke dope and get drunk. I had proudly obtained two tattoos on my upper arms, lost most contact with my family, turned my back on God and learned to hate anybody who I thought was a threat to me. My only mission was to survive another six months in-country and make it back to the States alive and physically fit. I did not think about the mental aspects of it. For this reason it would all come back to haunt me later in life.

One of the small pleasures of 1968 for me was that the Detroit Tigers baseball team advanced to the World Series against the St. Louis Cardinals. The games were carried on Armed Forces Radio Network, usually broadcast around two or three in the morning. I was an avid Tigers fan and I remember volunteering for the late watch simply so that I could turn on a small AM radio and hear the games. The Tigers won that year and I think I was the only Tigers fan in the entire Delta. Still, it was great to hear them win the 1968 World Series, a little slice of home right in the middle of a big ol' shithole.

The Mobile Riverine Force began to operate in new areas, areas our boat had not covered before. It was very late June and we hooked up with a small group of Green Berets who were heading; "in that direction." We had perhaps five river craft total. We went up small river canals lined by thick, nearly impenetrable jungle. There were several small encounters with the gooks but nothing major. Commander Sullivan was not aboard for this trip so the boat crew felt comfortable misbehaving any way they liked with no fear of disciplinary action. After four or five days of travel we came to a small village to unload the Green Berets. There was a big reception/picnic put together for us by the locals. We attended a food fest on the banks of the river. Then we learned that we were in actually in Cambodia and the Berets were on a secret search and destroy mission of some type. We were apparently deep into Cambodia. The second night back we anchored against the river bank, drew for the night watches, hunkered down and waited for daybreak. The crew had heard a story from the month previous that a riverboat crew had accidently strayed into Cambodia, was taken into custody and after a few weeks was released and eventually that crew was sent back to the states. That night we actually discussed this and had decided that it might be okay to be detained if we thought we would be sent home but after a few hours of drinking we decided it was not a thing we would let happen and the subject was dropped.

I had the first watch and sometime around midnight I went below and fell asleep. A few hours later I was shaken awake by another crewman and told to go topside where I found the whole crew just standing there quiet. I asked what was going on. I was told that sometime in the early morning hours that the boat broke free from its mooring when the tide started to rise and that the boat has been drifting with the river current back *deeper into Cambodia*. We had separated from the other boats and the boat captain had no clue where we were or how far we had drifted. This sense of hopelessness came upon me and I thought that maybe we are in huge danger; all eyes were on our captain for a solution to this problem. We stared at him, waiting for his command. He decided to start the engines and creep back in the direction we came from and hope we could find our way back to the other boats. He decided not to use the radios until sunrise. He hoped the engine noise would not cause us to become an open target on the river.

The river was very narrow and had lots of lazy turns. We took our weapon stations as the boat slowly headed off. At sunrise the captain got on the radio and made contact with the other boats, they were a few miles ahead of us and they wanted to know where the hell we had been? We finally caught up with them and thankfully no harm, no foul. So after spending another night in historic old Cambodia we headed back towards Vietnam.

Still, how does a soldier or seaman get "trained" to be lost with an entire crew of a boat in some foreign country that we were not supposed to be in? Answer, there is no training for it. You just try to think yourself out of this internationally dangerous and embarrassing situation! Again, my dumb luck was holding.

The first week of July we were in Long An Province and contact with Charlie was more frequent and much heavier as the summer wore on. We were involved in a large operation with many short duration firefights.

Then on July 3rd we were in a firefight for our lives. Contact with the enemy was heavy and the boats turned into the fire to unload their troops. Air support from the Cobra gunships was called in. It was a non-stop gun battle from sunrise onward when something very weird happened. One of the gunships was at treetop level when it received heavy enemy gunfire and the Cobra dropped into the middle of the river, shot down. This was not the first gunship I saw get shot down, but what was unusual was that within a half hour there were a half of dozen Navy frogman diving over the wreck to retrieve the fallen crew. The frogmen were diving during the firefight and everybody knew this was highly unusual to recover a crew in the middle of a massive firefight. The firefight raged on. Later, when the fight calmed down, we learned that General Westmorland's (Commander of US military operations in South Vietnam), brother-in-law was aboard the Cobra. It was very bizarre to witness divers in the middle of a firefight raging around them, diving to pull the crew from the chopper in very swift river currents.

A few of the boats were outfitted as medevac boats. These had a very small landing platform attached to the top of the boat that was just big enough to accommodate the choppers skids. It took great skill of the chopper pilot to safely land on the moving medevac boat, stay stable as the bird was loaded with the wounded and dead, and then depart safely. The medevac choppers had a large red cross painted on the underbelly and the sides of the helicopter to let everybody know that they were medical evacuation choppers, but the gooks regularly fired on the choppers landing and taking off from the medevac boats anyway. I believe using the medevac boat was how the fallen chopper crew was evacuated from the area. I can remember the bird lifting off from the boat and green tracer fire erupting from the gooks as the chopper made a radical takeoff to avoid the enemy fire.

CHAPTER 11

NEARLY THE LAST BREATH

In August RAS 112 was part of a large operation in and around the U Minh Forest, a stronghold for the VC for many years. There were many firefights and casualties during the operation, but the one firefight I will never forget was almost my last breath of life. That day was only one of a small handful of times that I asked God to get me through and give me the strength to carry on.

We had been out on the operation for many days and had many contacts with Charlie, some firefights bigger than others. Our crew had been very lucky since we'd arrived months before. The only real trouble was the boat captain having been replaced due to being a drunk and a mental midget. I knew that time was against us though. The longer we stayed out, the more of a chance there was that one or more of us would become a casualty of war.

On the morning of August 18, 1968, while operating on the Hai Muoi Tam canal, the VC initiated an RPG assault on the convoy, a full blown bad-ass ambush was about to commence. We had our usual compliment of 9th Infantry troops, along with the usual convoy of riverboats. It was early morning when we made the first contact with the enemy. As expected our command boat took an RPG rocket hit right at the waterline of the boat and we opened fire with all we had. Also as expected, the decision was made for the Tangos to head into the fire and drop the troops to seek and destroy the enemy forces.

The command boat and the gunboats held their ground and supplied covering fire for the troops off-loading onto the river bank. Once again our boat took another RPG hit just behind the command center and it slammed into our supply of small arms ammunition and C4 explosives stored in a small locker area. Unaware of this, we continued to fire as directed by the boat captain. The fear of running out of shells had never been a concern before, as the boat was well supplied with every type of ammo we used. I had a large supply of loaded clips to feed into the cannon. Below the cannon there were many more cans of loaded clips that were ready to be handed up to me if I ran low. The cannon crew was informed by the captain that we were now receiving RPG fire from the opposite side of the river. We were directed to fire in that direction while still holding our position on the river. The canal was narrow and enemy bunkers lined both sides of the river bank, shielded by heavy jungle. Our cannon shells were bunker busters, but the bunkers were hard to spot. The captain informed us that our fire was accurate and we were slamming the shells into the enemy bunkers. We continued to fire as directed.

This action went on for well over two hours and the heat and humidity inside the cannon turret was overwhelming. For the first time ever I was low on shell clips, so I yelled down below for more clips to be handed up to supply the cannon. The boat had taken two RPG rounds plus hundreds of small arm rounds that harmlessly bounced off the gun turret's heavy armor. I could still hear those rounds pinging off of the turret which told me there were perhaps hundreds of VC firing at the convoy. I assumed that the Army had been off-loaded by then and they too must have been under heavy enemy fire. They had stalled near the river bank and could not intrude into the jungle, there was just too much VC resistance.

My Italian friend was below shuttling up fresh clips to me to load into the cannon as we listened to the firefight outside the cannon turret raging on. Within the hour he yelled up at me with this look of desperation on his face to tell me we are almost out of ammo! There was only one full can of 40mm shells remaining, this would be the first time we had expended all of our shells and there was no end in sight to this firefight. I looked down at him directly into his eyes. He was soaked in sweat and he was physically spent. Then he says something that was desperate and depressingly hopeless, he says; "Let's get out of here." If his statement hadn't been so damned stupid it would have been funny! I think "Where in the hell are we going to go?" I was incarcerated in this hot as hell, metal cell, called a cannon turret, and I was doing hard time. The only way out that very minute was death. I was scared that a RPG was going to slam into the turret and end all of my misery in a nano-second and I would be on my way to the *real* hell! I was worn out and mentally shot, I had never been in a firefight this long without a break in the action. The fuckin' gooks were resisting everything the convoy could throw at them. The gunships above could not seem to break their ranks. I felt a sense of total defeat and for the first time desperation had set in. What this boat crew needed was a break, no not a break, but a miracle to get us out of there.

Then something unexpected happened. A message from the boat captain crackled over the headphones. Little did I know that something was about to happen to get the entire crew off the boat. A miracle? Not fucking likely! The RPG that hit behind the command center hours before had started a slow burning fire and the ammo and C4 stored there was ready to ignite. The 40mm cannon was out of commission, totally out of ammo. Suddenly there was a muffled explosion and I thought my fears that an RPG would slam into our turret had finally come true.

The boat captain screams into the headset for the cannon crew to get out of the turret! I didn't need to be told twice and jumped out onto the deck of the boat. What I saw next was pure chaos on the river. The noise was deafening. A flotilla of helicopter gunships were firing rocket rounds at the tree lines and bunkers. Savage short range firefights were coming from each boat. I smelled smoke, like burning, electrical type smoke, and as I turned to look at the back of the boat I saw thick, black smoke coming from the interior of our vessel. We were only 20 or 30 yards from the river bank and the boat captain ordered the coxswain to head straight in that direction. The boat was seriously damaged and the two engines were sputtering. The fear was that the boat would explode, so the crew needed to get off ASAP. The entire flotilla was in disarray and spread out on the river. The captain felt that heading for the river bank was our best option, as opposed to getting immediate help from another boat. He reasoned that the 9th Infantry troops we unloaded were somewhere near the river bank, if nothing else we could hook up with them for safety. I felt totally naked on the deck of the boat, exposed to the gooks who were pouring fire in at each boat in the convoy. I heard small arm rounds ricocheting off of the armor plating of the boat! I was not in a safe place. We were exposed in the open and I would rather take my chances on the river bank.

The boat was blowing thick black smoke as we reached the river bank. We jumped off hoping the boat would not explode beneath us. There were small arms fire and RPG rounds directed at us from the other side of the river, so we hunkered down on the muddy river bank, trying desperately to avoid the incoming fire. Two or three RPG's landed within feet of us. I put my arms over my head trying to protect my body from the flying shrapnel. In our haste to evacuate the boat we failed to secure any weapons, except for the coxswain who grabbed his

M-16 rifle. Great! Seven men and one M-16 between us. The boat captain directed us to run for cover into the jungle to avoid the fire in the hopes of finding the infantry. After we ran in only 100 feet or so there were no friendlies in sight, we had no radio to contact the flotilla or anybody else. It appeared we were doomed.

I could hear the gooks in the tree tops yelling at each other as they tried to zero in on us for target practice. The captain decides we need to go further in to find the infantry. We sprinted through heavy jungle another 30 or 40 yards then stumbled across this huge bomb crater half-filled with rancid, dark brown water. All seven of us dive head first into the crater as small arms fire whizzed over our heads. I landed face first into the murk and mud and decided to stay low with only my head above the water. There are no Army troops anywhere to be seen.

The crater stinks of filth and the first thought that comes to my mind is my SERE training back in California, "DO NOT allow yourself to become a POW under any circumstances." 'Shit, we're fucked, we're fucked, we're fucked!' is all I can think, as the gook chatter gets louder. I can picture one of them standing on the edge of the crater and mowing us down like ducks in a pond.

The coxswain has his M-16 trained out there somewhere, hoping maybe to get off a shot if he sees anything, while the rest of us were cowering in the muck. Everybody looks to the boat captain for direction and a solution to this mess we find ourselves in. What the captain decided would be the difference between life, capture or death. In the distance I can hear that the firefight is still raging on. We are stuck in a muddy hell hole with no apparent way out. For the moment at least all of us were alive.

They say there are no atheists in a fox-hole. That's exactly where I was, in a filthy, rank smelling fox hole carved out of the jungle by a bomb. I do not remember praying to God like you might see in a bad war movie; "Dear God, get me out of this and I will go to church every Sunday for the rest of my life, amen!" I did pray hard for some help right then though. The only thing I wanted was leadership from the captain. He needed to make a decision right there and then, instead he was silent.

I remember thinking about my grandmother who had passed three years prior. I had no reason why she popped into my mind, but I found comfort in thinking about her at that moment. Maybe she was there with me, I do not know. I had no sense of the time of day but I did know that I did not want to be in this crater after sunset. I suggested to the crew that making a run for the river was better than waiting for the AK-47 bullets that were sure to come. I did not think of my family or the tight bond I had with the crew. I thought that this might be the end of my life, yet I did not feel 100% panicked either. I just wanted to try something to get the hell out of that crater before it was too late.

The talk between the crew was minimal. The captain was now verbally trying to come up with a plan to save our asses. The chatter from the trees was clearly getting louder as Charlie had figured out that we probably had no way to defend ourselves. We had been stuck in this stink-hole crater for too long now and I'd had enough. I looked at the others and whispered that I was heading back to the river; I would rather be dead than to become a POW. I slowly inched my way to the top of the crater rim and had a look. I was soaking wet, smelled like a sewer and my boots were so lightly laced that I had trouble keeping them on my feet. The rest of the crew voiced no opposition, they joined me in looking over the rim of the crater.

It seemed clear. I tell myself that it is now or never and I jump to my feet and start the sprint through the jungle back towards the river. Small arms fire erupts around me and I hit the deck, jump up and sprint, hit the deck again, trying desperately to avoid the gook's fire. At this point I become totally stone deaf and do not hear any sounds around me, if the gooks are still firing at me I do not hear the rounds. The firefight from the direction of the river goes silent in my ears. I'm not aware that the crew is running with me, I'm only focused on reaching the river and hopefully finding a boat that can save our souls. I run and run and run and suddenly through the trees I see the water of the river and there it was, a Tango boat, 30 to 40 yards out from the river bank. I look around and see the whole crew together on the bank and without hesitation I kick off my boots. We all dive into the river, frantically swimming towards the boat; I can see the truck tire bumpers hanging from the side of the boat and I aim for one of them. If I can reach that tire, I can pull myself up to the deck of the boat and to safety. I'm physically dog tired but I push on against the river current and I can see a boat crewman yelling at his coxswain to reverse engines and slow down, we had been spotted.

I pulled myself up on the tire and a crewman extended his hand, pulling me onto the deck of the boat. I sprinted towards the well of the boat where the combat troops sat when being transported. I had no idea if troops were onboard or not. I ran to the back bulkhead of the compartment and put my back against the bulkhead and slowly slid down till I was sitting on the deck. I had my head down between my knees. I was physically spent, gasping for air. Now, finally I could hear the rest of my crew gathering near the bulkhead with me. All of us were struggling for breath and there was little talking, no hi-fives, no "glad to see ya made its."

I finally looked up and gazed straight ahead when it hit me; we were on the body/medical boat, the boat that had collected, bagged and tagged all the KIA's. They were stacked in rows right in front of me. When I ran into the well of the boat I was running across those bags to get to the back bulkhead and I realized I had just run across the bodies of fallen Army and Navy personnel. Our crew, all seven of us, could have easily been in that stack.

The only injury to our crew was the coxswain who took an AK-47 round to his arm on the run out. Odd, the one guy with a rifle is shot, the rest of us unarmed, came out without a scratch. Other than that, we all made in back in one piece. I thought to myself that even though I was grateful for the outcome we were not out of the woods yet, as the firefight continued on around us, bullets, grenades and bombs ripping through the jungle and men's bodies.

Sometime afterwards, nearing nightfall, the firefight finally came to an end. We were taken back to our boat, sitting right where we left it. The fire was out but the boat was a mess. The engines where dead so we were towed by another boat and I all I did was just sit and think what could have been.

It was dark as we wound our way out of this hellish area of death and destruction. The beaten down convoy encountered some small resistance by Charlie, but we made it back safely and our boat went into dry dock for repairs. The summer of 1968 was coming to a close and I felt lucky to be alive and in one piece. But shit, I still had five months to go and only God knew what was in store for me and my crew.

CHAPTER 12

ACCEPTING ABNORMAL AS NORMAL

There are sayings like "The fog of war" or "War is hell" that I had heard long before I got to Vietnam but the fact is those phrases are very close to the truth. When I first arrived in-country my brain could not comprehend some of the things that I had witnessed. I was thousands of miles from home. Outside of a death in my family I had never seen a dead body or even come close to witnessing violence on any level. As my tour marched on and the days passed by, my brain had sadly grown to accept the hundreds of scenes of violence I was seeing. Each one I took in I saw as a daily possibility for me and my crew. Even worse, I got to the point that a dead body in any condition did not faze me, unless the body was an American, any American of any color. I actually was able to justify in my mind the sight of a dead and butchered body of the "enemy" as okay, but to see a dead American was always horrifying to me. You became numb to the violence around yourself and the only thing that mattered was self-preservation. "Better them than me" becomes your motto. Some handle this mental anguish better than others. I would put myself somewhere in the middle of the scale. I didn't need alcohol or dope every day to function but I did use some stimulants on a regular basis to get through some of the shit I witnessed, so I was no saint.

I knew what the term "Million Dollar Wound" meant before I arrived in Vietnam. It is the very lucky combat wound that will likely get you a free ticket home prior to the end of your tour. Wounds such as becoming temporarily blind from a flash grenade; or mangling your shooting hand so bad you can no longer pull the trigger of an M16 rifle; or maybe taking a bullet to a knee so you can no longer walk until you have reconstructive surgery. All of these wounds were painful in the beginning but with the proper therapy back in the world you could go on with a happy, productive life. I personally never witnessed anybody receiving this wound but there were men who were always thinking to maybe, just maybe, come up with a plan to manufacture the elusive Million Dollar Wound.

To make this point, one night we were moored on the river and a bunch of us were playing poker. Some guy from another crew jumped over to our boat. He wanted to talk to any member of the 40mm cannon crew. I was the only one from that crew there, so I asked what he wanted. He begins to tell us that he has had it with this "shit" and he had figured out a way to get sent home. He asked me how much a full case of 40mm shell clips weighed. I started to think about that, there were 4 shells to a clip and each can carried 4 clips or 16 shells, well anyway the full can was pretty heavy. I told him I didn't know, maybe 60 to 100 lbs each, why? He tells us that he would greatly appreciate it if someone, (he was talking directly to me), would hold that can maybe 6 feet above his arm and let the can go, smashing his arm in the processes. *What*? Who would do something like that? And how could he possible know that the injury would be severe enough to get him sent back to the world for treatment? I politely told him no and suggested that he take a hit of the opium and go back to his boat. Somebody near us pipes up and says; "I'll do it!" The guy gets really excited and puts his arm flat on the deck and tells this other guy to get the case and do it. The guy goes down below and brings up one sealed case of 40mm clips, walks over to where the other guy is laid out on the deck, raises the can above his head and without hesitation lets the can drop. *Lordy! Lordy!* A *massive* scream comes from the injured sailor! We get some flashlights so we can we look at his arm. It looks like a roller coaster track, twisted and cracked in 3 or 4 places. The only words I hear from anybody is "Medic!" and "Man! That was cold!" Shortly a group of Army guys show up, perform some basic treatment on his arm and walk him away to what I can only I assume is a field hospital. He was crying in agony with the pain.

We resumed our poker game like this stupid incident never happened. I did hear some weeks later that he was flown to a hospital and was recovering in-country. I guessed he did not get the Million Dollar Wound that he was hoping for.

One of the concerns I still have 40 plus years after serving in Vietnam is Agent Orange. This was an aerial defoliation program known as "Operation Ranch Hand," used by the military. The goal was to defoliate rural and forested land, by spraying Agent Orange from planes throughout Vietnam. I remember seeing a plane spraying this stuff and nobody was told to take cover or to avoid it during the spraying. The military figured if they could kill the jungle, then Charlie had nowhere to hide and it would be easier to find him. What nobody told the troops or the civilians on the ground was that Agent Orange was deadly to humans.

Sadly, my understanding now is that it can stay in your system for years before it kicks in and kills you or gives you cancer. I'm sure sometime during my time in Nam I breathed in the stuff. I was recently asked by the Veteran's Administration if I wanted to be tested for Agent Orange toxicity. I turned them down. Still, I have wondered over the years if it is indeed in my system and if it will ever take hold, I don't lose sleep over it but I do think about it.

The chief of naval operations in Vietnam in 1968 was Admiral Elmo Zumwalt. He was the one who really ramped up combat operations involving riverboats and the aggressive use of Agent Orange in the Mekong Delta. Zumwalt's son had volunteered for riverboat duty and was the captain of a swift boat operating in the areas ordered sprayed with Agent Orange by his father. Later he became ill from the effects of this poisonous defoliant and died in 1988. A sad twist of fate for the son of a man who thought deforestation was the answer to ending the war. Talk about being on the Dark Side of the Moon where ignorance is bliss. I wonder if Zumwalt ever told his son how dangerous this stuff was? Did he even care? Vietnam was a war where the darkness and ignorance continued to claim and still claims casualties, long after our American troops had left the battlefield.

I had awhile to go before I left the battlefield though. It sucks being away from your family at an early age. It doubly sucks when you have a 50/50 chance you might be dead by the end of each new day. For me to watch the people I trained and lived with all those months change before my very eyes because of this fear, was, well it was an eye opener. Some guys were very even tempered to start, others not so much. The one common thing between us all, after months in-country, was the learned ability to witness tragedy and feel no sympathy for the fallen or down-trodden of the enemy.

Even seeing the little kids and the women that lived in poverty and filth had little effect on me. If I had seen this while living back in Phoenix I would have felt horrible for those people and would have done something to help out. But in Vietnam it did not even cross my mind. I have some 8mm film of myself and a couple of other crew members teasing a group of young South Vietnamese boys with scraps of leftovers from a couple of boxes of c-rations. We threw the scraps out onto the filthy, muddy river bank and watched and laughed with glee as a dozen or so boys 7 or 8 years old fought for them. They pushed and shoved each other in the mud to grab packets of salt and sugar and we thought that this was great sport, so great that I filmed it. We then supplied these young boys with cigarettes and howled with laughter as they smoked and hammed it up for the camera while a pregnant girl with a toddler in her arms watched from a few feet away. Remember, these were our allies, the people we were protecting from the VC. I thought nothing of it at the time. In fact I never really gave it much thought until many years later, when it slowly came to me that I was *not* the same person then as I was before and after I left Vietnam.

Most days "in the shit" you just didn't give a crap about much of anything except making it to the next day. I would much rather have been on a mission, staying busy, than to sit around for maybe a week waiting for the next operation. I did not want the down time, because that is when I would get depressed thinking too much about stuff. Sometime maybe halfway through my tour while we were in Dong Tam, I was told to report to an administration building on the base, I had no clue what this was about but I did what I was told. When I got there I was told I was up for a promotion. They said that sometime in the next 30 days I needed to take the written promotional test. Then, hopefully there would be a slot opening up for me to fill for a higher pay grade position.

At the time I was classified as an E-3 boatswain's mate, which wasn't too high up the ladder for someone who had been in the Navy for nearly 3 years. Of course I had been demoted just before I came to Vietnam. Then reinstated when I got processed in-country. However, I immediately got defensive and asked why I was not getting an automatic field promotion in a combat zone? I was told the Navy didn't give out field promotions. Again they told me I needed to take a written test for the promotion. I had seen Army guys come to Vietnam right after boot camp as an E-2, within 6 months they are field promoted to E-3 & 4's. I protested the fact that I had to take the written test. They told me to take it or leave it and I told them, in a very mature 20 year old way, "fuck off, I ain't taking no test." I was never again invited to take the written test and left Vietnam an E-3.

This was an example of the abnormal becoming normal on the dark side of the moon. In the regular blue water navy I would have never dreamed of talking to any other sailor with the vulgar attitude I had that day. Further, the personnel towards whom I directed the words would have put me on report, and I most assuredly would have gone to Captain's Mast for punishment. At this point I was slowly losing all sense of proper behavior, especially around other sailors of higher rank, and the sad part was I did not even notice the change. Even worse, I didn't care.

The boats rarely traveled at night as a convoy but it did happen occasionally. One night late, the convoy was slowly traveling on a narrow river with jungle on both banks. I was at my post in the 40mm turret. I had the turret hatch open and was simply watching the trees go by in the dark, when I noticed the convoy entering a small village situated on the river bank. I saw some dim lights coming from a few of the thatched huts. I spotted some chickens running loose. It seemed peaceful and serene. There were perhaps half a dozen sampans docked on the river bank. Then I heard the crack of an AK47 rifle coming from the village. I looked up river and I spotted a few green tracer rounds being fired at the boat ahead of ours. I slammed the hatch door shut. Within seconds the boat captain ordered all guns to commence firing. The canon was already cocked and loaded and the 40mm came to life as we started to fire.

When you found yourself in this situation you simply did what you were ordered and didn't ask any questions. You figured that surely the brains of the outfit must have known something we did not. So we fired as ordered. It was clear by the noise around me that all of the boats in the convoy had opened fired on this village as we moved along at a snail's pace. The convoy continued to fire for 5 or 6 minutes until the captain gave the order to cease fire. I was aware that there was little or no return fire from the village so I opened the turret hatch to see the tail end of the village burning to the ground! The convoy never stopped to investigate. We moved on like nothing happened. A few green tracer rounds, probably from a sniper, was enough justification to level that village. The number of women and children killed or left homeless was unknown. The boat's captain never briefed us on this action and I do not think anybody ever asked about it. This war had become fucking stupid and senseless. However, it took me many more months to realize that the war was running the Generals, the Generals were not running the war.

One time we did an operation with a group of very aggressive Korean marines (ROK), who operated these two man swamp boats powered by large fans positioned on the tail of a boat. These were similar to the ones you see in the Louisiana Bayous or Florida swamps. They are like hover craft they go so fast. They can cruise over bits of land, or stands of swamp grass with ease. One marine would operate the boat and the other would man a .50 caliber machine gun on the bow of the boat. These sick little bastards loved to chase the gooks across rice paddies and mow them down or chase them into the tree lines and they did an excellent job of it.

The ROK's stayed to themselves and it was well known they did not bring back prisoners alive. The prisoners might start out alive, but they never ended up that way.

One day we were with a group of ROK's on a very small river and they had just rounded up a group of 6 or 7 VC. They had them lined up on the riverbank so that their commander could interrogate them. I was sitting right next to my 40mm turret about 100 feet away and was watching the commander ask the VC some questions through an interpreter. The 5' tall ROK commander was very loud and animated. He was becoming very agitated as the first two VC in line were not answering his questions, he was going back and forth between the two VC with no luck. The commander pulled out his sidearm and started to scream at the group of VC which in turn made the interpreter scream as well. I remember that all movements from the ROK commander became like slow motion as he put the pistol to the head of the first VC in the line. It was like I knew that he was going to kill this guy and my brain could not compute fast enough to keep up with the action my eyes saw. I hear a pop long before my brain lets me see what happens. The VC falls backwards down the muddy riverbank and lands at the edge of the water. Like a well-rehearsed chorus line, the remaining prisoners all start to scream information the commander had demanded. The psycho nut-job commander actually pulled the trigger on an unarmed man. Just executed him on the spot. Full of himself, he lights up like a Christmas tree with delight and marches the other prisoners out of sight down the riverbank. I just sat there not knowing what to think. Honestly I don't even think I brought up the incident to the rest of my crew later that day. Deadly violence like that numbs your brain and muddies your normal thought process. Still, I quickly recovered and continued on with my day. Yet these scenes sunk in, packed away in my subconscious mind, where they began to do some damage.

Sometime during the next day the boats were staging on the river bank of this small canal. We were all just waiting around for the commanders to give us the word to shove off. The area we were in was surrounded by thick jungle. Just in front of our boat was a small clearing where a platoon of the crazy little ROK bastards from Korea were also waiting. I noticed a young Vietnamese man sitting with the ROK's in typical VC clothing. He had a crude tattoo on his hand. I knew what the tattoo signified; he was a former VC who flipped to the side of the ARVN's and was no longer fighting for the VC. The normal course of action for someone who flips is to go out on patrol with the ARVN's, or any allied unit, and walk point without a weapon, to prove his loyalty to the South Vietnamese government. Walking Point meant he was the first in line on the patrol, but with no weapon or even a helmet, his chances of living through the operation were not too good. He might go out two or three times this way until the ARVN commanders felt that he was not a threat to his troops and he would eventually be given a weapon to fight with.

I saw an interpreter standing close by and I asked this guy if he knew the story behind the former VC and why he flipped. He laughed out loud and told me this story; He was not a VC but a NVA soldier from up north near the DMZ. Many months ago he was loaded down with a backpack full of RPG rounds. He was then told to go by foot south and deliver them to a specific point in the Mekong Delta, which he did. After many months of hiking south on the Ho Chi Minh trail and dodging his enemies, he reached his drop-off point. There he was told to turn around and go back and get some more RPG's. However you say "fuck you" in Vietnamese is what he told them, and he flipped to the other side. The interpreter roared with laughter and slapped me on the back and the insanity continued.

Since smoking dope was part of my life at this time it was not unusual to try different ways to get high. A most unique and very effective way was a technique called "shotgunning." You first obtain a break-action shotgun and after breaking open the breach, the smoker would put the barrel of the shotgun in his mouth and the other guy blows opium from the break point, down the barrel, as the guy with the barrel in his mouth sucks in air as fast as he can. This caused the opium to rush into your lungs and in theory, gave you this massive high. I was only on the receiving end of the barrel a couple of times and I must say I got a buzz quickly. Still, I had this creepy feeling of having a gun barrel in my mouth, so I moved on from shotgunning.

As the end of the year came near I was actually looking towards the future and I drastically cut back on the use of opium. Mainly because of the fear that if I did make it home, the last thing I needed was a dependency on drugs, as there would be no way of me hiding that from my family. How did I break the opium habit? I just went cold-turkey. Really, it was harder for me to quit cigarettes than opium.

One night along the way we had a few down days and we spent a few nights sleeping on the base at Dong Tam. This was a nice break from sleeping every night on the boat. I remember that Dong Tam did get their fair share of in-coming rounds, not like the barrage of rounds we experienced in I Corps, but they did have in-coming. This night there were some in-coming rounds and so I headed for a group of bunkers not far from where we were sleeping. I dove into the first bunker I came across and there were maybe 8 or 9 guys already in there. I quickly found myself a spot to wait out the bombardment. This event normally did not cause me much alarm, as an in-coming round would have to hit your bunker with a direct hit to cause any damage. What were the odds of that? So I was in the bunker less than 20 minutes when I heard a commotion coming from outside. I got out of the bunker to take a look. I saw a lot of men milling about near the entrance of the bunker next to the one I was in. I thought maybe a round had hit the bunker and there were injuries. Instead I was told that there was a shooting inside the bunker and someone was killed. This is where "the fog of war" really is defined. You seek out a bunker for protection from bombs and rockets and instead you are killed inside the bunker by a "friendly," a soldier or sailor like yourself.

There was this problem with race the whole time I was in Vietnam, the Blacks hung out with Blacks, the Whites hung out with Whites. If you were a different color than that, then you would just have to try and find someplace to fit in. I had zero problems with any other race. I often hung with a group of Blacks that I befriended back in training. But there was always a pressure by other Whites not to mix too heavily with Blacks, except when we were on operations.

Working together like that was apparently okay. Because like we were all on the same job and we all needed each other to survive. We were all going to kill the gooks together as one big happy unit. But on your off time you were pressured to stay with your own kind. It was all such bullshit.

So back in the bunker it turns out that a White guy had an argument with this Black guy and the White guy shot the Black guy with his sidearm, killing him. The questions arose in my mind: What other dysfunctional crap am I going to see in this screwed up place??? How can one American shoot another American in a bunker with shells falling all around them? What kind of racists, psychos and other screwed up people were not only fighting in, but like Old Man Sullivan, probably running this war? I chalked up this experience as another one for the books and went on with my day.

I rarely got mail and I rarely wrote home. I knew one thing for sure, I would *never* put any of this in a letter as my family back home would think I was making it all up. Nobody would believe some of the things that I had seen. What I didn't know was that back home, a lot of this stuff was coming to light, and the war and the military men fighting it were becoming more and more unpopular because of it.

My nature was naturally gregarious and I liked to talk to anybody I met. I always asked questions, because I was always curious as to what someone else thought about life in general. When we were on an operation in I Corps, working with the 3rd Marine division, I saw a guy walking along where the boats were moored and he was carrying a long rifle with a large scope that did not look military issued. He was not too much older than me, so I asked him what kind of rifle he was carrying. He told me what is was. I asked if that type of weapon was issued by the U.S. Marine Corps. He shook his head no. He came over and we shared a cigarette. He proceeded to tell me that he was a sniper and he and his partner had just got off a multi-day mission somewhere north of the DMZ. I was immediately intrigued, so I asked all of these questions about his job. Without many names or details he told me that he and his partner were dropped by chopper into the jungle. They hiked for three or four days to find their target. Then they hid away for another day preparing, finally zeroing in on the target from atop a small hill, among some boulders. He got a bead on the target, his spotter gave him all of the information he needed and he pulled the trigger, hitting and killing the target at long range. They then made their way back to the pick-up point, were picked up by the chopper and flown back to their point of origin. He thanked me for the cigarette and went on his way, just another nameless face and another day at the office.

Every day could bring some fresh, new, dark-side craziness for us to witness. One day I saw a little man who was an ARVN commander, set fire to the beard of an elder civilian who could not answer his questions fast enough. The commander, laughing like a little school girl, got excited when the flames reached the man's skin, just another example of the nut jobs running this insanity.

Another time I saw a helicopter crewman who, after landing on the small pad on a converted riverboat, lost his balance after leaving the chopper. The blade of the chopper cut his arm off and began spinning the guy like a top! I'm not sure if he survived or not. It was a lot like fast forwarding a movie on your DVR, the scenes in my head could not keep up with the reality I was seeing.

On one operation a chopper came in fast and low over a small group of civilian huts and blew the homes off their foundations just like a tornado would do. The villagers came running after the landing chopper and demanded to be compensated for their loss. The chopper pilot asked one of us to grab a couple cases of C-rats and give them to the villagers. We did, and the whole group of civilians smiled with pleasure with the two cases and they went on their way. Was this what a group of houses was worth in this country, two cases of C-rats? Yep!

Just like in several Vietnam films of the present day, I participated in taking pot-shots at farmers working in their rice paddies, not knowing if they were the enemy or not. Fortunately we did not hit anybody. At the time it seemed like the right thing to do, just randomly shooting at people in the distance. I think my time there had hardened my heart and my judgment. Still, after every mandatory memorial service for our dead, I would justify my actions because so many Americans were dying weekly and I wanted to do my fair share to defeat the enemy. So I continued on like this week after week. Each day bringing me closer to mustering out, or being blown to pieces someone might fish out of a river.

My worst nightmare scenario, the one that kept me in a constant state of fear, happened during what was kind of an average firefight. I heard this thudding noise right outside of the turret. I yelled down to the pointer and asked if he had heard the thud and he nodded yes. Shortly afterwards the firefight was over, we climbed out of the turret to find a B-40 RPG rocket lying on the deck of the boat at the base of the cannon turret. The thud was a dud! The RPG rocket that had been shot at us, had failed to explode on impact on the cannon turret. It had dropped harmlessly to the deck of the boat. You could see where the rocket hit the turret and it was just about level with where my head would have been on the other side of the steel. I had just come as close to the same fate as my friend Doug Morton had as I could have come. A rocket to the side of the head. Now, you would think that I would have said a prayer, thanking God for the rocket being a dud. But I don't think I did. I just stared at the rocket and thought about what could have been. You would think that I would have fallen to my knees and raised my hands to the heavens thanking God for this small miracle, for sparing my life once again. Hell maybe even thanking Doug's spirit for having saved me? Yet sadly, In reality, all I did was stare at the rocket lying on the deck and think of Doug Morton, wondering if he suffered any pain when it happened, wondering why him and not me?

I think I might have actually blamed God at this point, because I knew that in my lifetime I would *never know* why Doug had died and not me. I might have been, in retrospect, really upset with God for just about everything.To say that a war can screw your mind up is one thing but to witness it is something else.

Another abnormal event happened sometime within the last 60 days of my tour. The boat was having some minor maintenance done and we spent the night on the Dong Tam base. Most of the crew were drinking and playing cards. It was very late at night when an Army guy came into our barracks and started to walk towards us. He was wearing Army issued, jungle green fatigues and he was carrying an M-16 rifle, which I noticed did not have a clip in. He appeared agitated and he walked right up to the boat captain who was sitting next to me. We had been drinking most of the night but we were not drunk, all we were doing was playing a few hands of poker. He stood directly over the captain and demanded to know who was in charge. He wanted to know why our barracks was in such a mess and not ship shape. The captain looked up at him and said something to the effect of "fuck off," when this guy takes the butt of the M-16 and slams it to the side of the captain's head! He fell to the floor in obvious pain.

At that point I was thankful the guy did not have a clip in the M-16. We all jumped up from the table and the guy ran out of the barracks with all of us in hot pursuit. He made a right turn out the door. I could see his outline in the dark but he is a good 10 yards ahead of us, but the chase was on! I was second or third in line. We were all running pretty fast. Just as we gained on the guy I heard the unmistakable sound of a metal clip being slammed into the M-16! Somebody screamed that he was loading his weapon, just as the guy stops and turns around and takes aim at us. One of our guys tackled the guy at his knees before he had a chance to squeeze off some rounds . . . and it was over. Talk about death by friendly fire! How did this U.S. soldier become an enemy?

I was pretty sober by then and I ran back to the barracks to see if the captain was alright. He had a good sized gash on the side of his head, but he was okay and I was grateful for that. The MP's responded quickly and took the Army guy away. Later that night the MP's were back to get a statement from us and we were told that the guy simply "lost it," and that was about it. Still, attempted murder of fellow soldiers, because our barracks was dirty? Never heard another word about it again, but it certainly made me think how the human mind can be pushed only so far before it snaps. For some the snap was faster than for others.

On one very routine operation there was a break in the movements of the convoy. We were told that we were going to hunker down for the night and head out again early in the morning. Just before we positioned our boats for the overnight stay, there was the cracking noise of gun fire coming from the tree line, just across the narrow river from our location. Small arms fire was not normally a signal to panic. We all scoured the jungle to see if we could spot where the fire was coming from. Old man Sullivan was onboard the boat at that time and he said something to the effect of "fuck this!" and got on the radio and called for a Cobra gunship to do a fly over of the trees to see what was up. Within a few minutes the Cobra was flying low over the tree tops when the sounds of an AK47 opened up on the chopper. The pilot did a circle and came diving down with the chopper's 20mm Gatling guns blazing away in the direction of the AK47 fire. This was definitely a trip to watch, as the chopper was loud and deadly and everyone was amazed as the chopper pulled up and the AK47 rounds exploded again in the direction of the Cobra; the shooter was still active. The pilot made one more pass and the gunship pissed out even more fire power. Finally there was silence from the jungle.

Sullivan ordered a small contingent of troops to go in and do a quick sweep of the area. We watched them enter the jungle and minutes later reappear on the riverbank and give the thumbs up to Commander Sullivan. The shooter of the AK47 was a young, teenage girl who tried in vain to take down a Cobra gunship, they dragged her lifeless body out of the jungle and put her on the river bank, another Buddhist soul had entered Paradise after dying in combat.

CHAPTER 13

LIFE ON THE DARK SIDE OF THE MOON

Honestly the thing that I did like the most about my tour with the Mobile Riverine Force was the complete lack of discipline by my superiors. It was not like the regular Navy where pressed uniforms and obeying the regulations was expected and demanded. When I arrived in Vietnam I had a boot camp style haircut ordered by my Captain's Mast, but I never cut my hair once while I was in Vietnam. I went nearly a full year without so much as a trim. My hair at its longest went well past my collar well over my ears. I used to push my hair under this jungle green flop hat if I knew I was going to be around any brass, but most of the time I just let my hair grow and did not try to hide it. I wish I had been able to grow a beard in those days, because I would have had one of those too. But the long hair was great and the best part was that nobody seemed give a rat's ass that my hair was long. Nobody seemed to care about any regulations. You could go around shirtless, tucked in or not, wear any hat type you chose to put on, grow a mustache or beard in any style of your own choosing. The word "sir" was never used.

Unless you knew the person's rank you would have no idea who was what, since nobody wore patches to identify their rank, let alone what branch of the service they were in. I knew going back to the regular Navy after this tour of duty might be a real problem for someone like me, I loved the no-rules navy I found myself in.

Personal hygiene could be a challenge and swimming or bathing in the river water was a definite no. The things that floated in the water and the bacteria in those rivers could be a serious hazard to your health.

One very hot and humid day I just needed to cool off. I slipped into the river just to get some relief, I planned on staying in the water for only a minute or so and was just starting to pull myself out of the water when one of the crew starting laughing at me and pointed behind me. Right behind me, bobbing in the water, was a human head! I scrambled to get back on the boat to the laughter of the crew. Of course we collected the head and logged the find but this is why you stayed out of the river water, it was *nasty*.

If you were lucky enough to get caught in a massive monsoon rain storm it was your chance to finally get a fresh water shower. Not all would do what some of us did, as for me though as soon as this very hard rain would began to fall I would grab a bar of soap, strip naked and began my nature shower. Cool fresh water falling from the heavens was what I considered a gift, and I took advantage of it. Sadly there were times when the rain fell during an operation and I was unable to shower, but if I could I would and it felt extremely good. There were times when four or five naked guys were going down the river on the bow of the boat soaping up. It was a different world on the river.

One late afternoon after a day of no contact with the VC, the decision was made to hunker down on this small river for the night and resume the operation the next morning. This I quickly learned was a normal procedure for the convoy, as you did not want to be on these small treacherous rivers in the dark. A half hour or so before sundown three or four of us were on the bow of the boat near the 40mm turret smoking cigarettes, when somebody noticed a few small boats upriver crossing from one side to the other. These small boats were maybe 400 yards away and it was hard to tell who they were, friend or foe. Binoculars were used and somebody determined that the boats were full of VC trying to get to the other side of the river. How they knew they were VC I'll never know, as daylight was fading quickly. I certainly did not feel threatened by them, but a challenge was set forth and the 40mm crew accepted. We jumped in the turret and prepared to fire upriver at these small boats. The challenge was to get the cannon loaded and cocked and get a shot off before any of the boats could successfully cross the river. Now this was really dumb because the river was very narrow and it took a minute or so to get the cannon in firing position. By that time the boats might be able to cross long before we could get a shot off. Besides, we really didn't know who was in the boats crossing the river, it could be a family going on a picnic for all we knew.

However it seemed like fun at the time and we readied the cannon to fire. Little did we know, shut up in the cannon turret, that some gung-ho yahoo had got on a radio and was able to find a fighter jet that was in the area. He called in an air strike on the boats! We took aim and fired off three shots and waited for the spotter to give direction up or down, left or right. Instead what we heard was excitement on the deck of the boat. We climbed out of the turret and there wasn't one whole boat in the water, just pieces of wood pushed up against the riverbank.

Looking through the binoculars you could plainly see that all of the boats crossing over had been sunk. We jumped for joy with excitement. It had seemed more like a carnival midway game we were playing. Our cannon crew had just knocked over the weighted milk bottles with three shells. Someone should have given us the *big* teddy bear as a prize. Now that is what you call a hell of a good time in a war zone. Just some good natured fun.

While we were all still high fiving each other we hear the shrieking noise of a jet engine right over our heads as the fighter jet swoops down the river and releases a bomb on his target. It was a little too close for comfort, as the jet released the bomb too soon! They always pulled that crap! We all hit the deck with our arms over our heads hoping for the best but expecting the worst. The bomb went off and large chunks of shrapnel whistled over our heads and I heard a loud thud noise behind me . . . we got up to see a piece of red hot metal from the bomb had hit the side of one of the 20mm gun turrets and landed on the deck of the boat.

The carnival atmosphere was suddenly gone. They radioed the jet to back off and we went to look at the piece of metal that could have easily taken one of our heads off. The chunk of metal is sitting there and is visibly smoldering. It was way too hot to even kick it into the river to get rid of it. After a half hour we got a bucket of river water and we picked up the shrapnel with a metal tool, dropping it in the bucket. The water started to sizzle from the heat of the metal. No more carnival games for me. The sad part was that by now it had become dark and we never did investigate the boats we sank in the river. (So now you see why there might be a head or arm floating along the current while you are trying to take a bath). I felt pretty bad. I hoped it was not a family going on a picnic.

For someone as young as I was there were some things about the war zone that I thought were pretty "cool" at the time. There were many forms of high powered weapons that were used daily against the VC by us and the Army. For instance, to aid in the accuracy of guiding the shells to their target was the use of "tracer rounds." Tracers were a shell with a small explosive in their base. When the tracer exploded it would burn red in color. The tracer round was usually placed every 5th or 6th round in a machine gun belt. When there were thousands of rounds being fired each minute, the tracers would blend together so the fire coming from the weapon appeared to be a ribbon of red heading for the target being fired at. As I've mentioned before the tracer rounds used by the VC were green in color and were used for the same purpose. As I remember it, the fire coming from the VC's green tracers appeared to be placed further apart and the effect was more like a dotted line effect.

My very favorite piece of war machinery in the MRF was called the "Zippo," a converted ATC made into a floating flamethrower. I don't think there were many Zippos in the fleet but I did work with them on a few operations. They were amazing to work with. A Zippo carried hundreds of gallons of napalm and it was called into action for many different situations. One use was to cover suspected VC bunker clusters in napalm. My understanding was that the napalm did not have to make contact with a person to kill them. Once sprayed over a bunker, the fiery napalm sucks the oxygen right out of the bunker, causing anyone inside to suffocate. The Zippo had a short shot, maybe 30 seconds or so, but it did devastating work. It was a trip to see the napalm dripping off the trees and dropping onto the water and continuing to burn, it truly was an amazing sight.

My second favorite piece of deadly and devastating war machinery was "Puff the Magic Dragon," a fixed wing cargo plane converted into a gunship that used high powered Gatling guns. The plane would go in a slow tight circle and cover the target below with thousands of rounds ammo a minute and would level anything or anybody its path. I was able to see this monster at work a half a dozen times and it was really impressive at night when all you could see was a thin ribbon of red tracer fire coming from the guns onboard the plane and the thundering sounds of the shells exploding on contact.

When our crew took over C-112-1 the previous crew named the boat "The Maverick" which I thought was cheesy name, but we kept that name as it was painted on the side of the 20mm turret. We did however decide to paint one other thing on the 20mm turret. (With which I have pictures of myself proudly posing.) That was the words "SAT CONG" which means "kill communists." Sat Cong was a phrase the ARVN had come up with. Supposedly there was an award given by some ARVN commander to any of his troops who killed the VC. This was called a "Sat Cong badge." Plus the soldier got the privilege of tattooing those words on his chest. He had to earn that tattoo, kind of like the Japanese mafia. There were some hard core 9th infantry troops who also adopted the tattoo, but we decided the words on the 20mm turret were sufficient. Any little jab you could deliver to the enemy was always sought after, as this was our way of contributing to the war effort.

I want to make one thing very clear, I was in no more or less danger than any of the other troops who were in combat. Every man who fought in a firefight in Nam has their own stories to tell about went on around them. The difference with us, the Mobile Riverine Force, was that we were a very small specialized unit of regular Navy men who, for the most part, did not start their military careers right out of boot camp then straight into combat. Everybody, for the most part who served on the boats, was taken out of the regular Navy and molded into something they did not even know existed. Most sailors in this man's navy were not engaged in one on one firefights which could wind up with them being on the ground in close combat with the enemy. Most navy ships were used to bring in supplies, ammo, men and weapons, or to shell the enemy from a distance; usually very safe and even boring duties. The North Vietnamese didn't have a navy or an air force that could take on our ships. So being in the Blue Water Navy was pretty mundane. The Brown Water Navy was not the normal world of pressed dress white uniforms and overwhelming naval regulations to follow. Because of that I thought it might be impossible for me to integrate back into the formal naval service after serving my tour in Vietnam. I cannot really explain it but it was like not really being in the Navy, it was more like a job you took for a 12 month period where all of the work rules where abandoned and thrown out. As long as you did the job you were fine. The "office managers" let you do what you wanted to do on your off time. Yes I was serving in the military but not in the Navy that I was accustomed to. By the time my 12 months were up I was ready to cut ties with the Navy and go my own way. I suppose I felt superior to the other sailors who had not served on the Brown Water boats. I felt that combat had earned me a special spot in the Navy but I knew that the Navy did not feel that way about me.

As the summer of 1968 turned into fall I had actually seriously considered extending my tour in Vietnam for one more year. The only thing was that when I did leave Vietnam I would be discharged out of the military and I could return home. If I did another year in Vietnam I would have to extend my Navy service for at least another couple of years and I wasn't sure I wanted to do that. Another year in Vietnam was do-able but another year after that in the regular Navy was not appealing. I ran into maybe three guys who either had already extended their riverboat duty or were about to. I thought about it for many weeks before deciding one year was enough. Besides, there were rumors floating around that the MRF might be dismantled or turned over to the Vietnamese Navy in its entirety, so the future of the Brown Water boats was in question. So I decided not to make a career out of the Navy. I was going to go back to the States and muster out of the military.

I'm not the sharpest tool in the shed, but I have to say I seemed to be surrounded by real mental midgets every hour of every day while I was on tour in Nam. I truly liked every man on my boat crew but there were times I wondered how some of them would make it through life outside of the Navy.

One crewman constantly talked about how wonderful his wife was, even though he would receive letters from her that would put him in a rage, letters telling him not to believe the rumors about her when he returned home, or how much she enjoyed the movies the other night with the neighbor's divorced husband. These things would drive this guy nuts. He was to meet her in Hawaii for R & R and he was all jacked up about that. His R & R time arrived and he departed for Hawaii. A week or so later he arrived back on the boat. He told us he'd had a great time, that his wife was especially wonderful on the visit and that he had a "real treat" for the crew. He gathered us in a circle and he pulled out a dozen or so black and white Polaroid photos and starts to pass them around one photo at a time. I kid you not, the first photo is a picture of his wife fully clothed sitting on a couch in his hotel room and she is wearing a very pleasant smile (I don't want to say she was ugly but she was not what you would call a looker.) Each photo after that showed the wife with one less piece of clothing until the last picture showed her naked on the couch with her legs spread wide open. This guy is staring at us with a big smile, waiting for a reaction from the crew. I mean what is this moron thinking? This is the "real treat" that will tickle the crew? If I was from the backwoods of the hill country and I was married to my sister I would have been pleased as punch. But it was like, total silence from the crew. I looked around at everybody else and this is when the laughter started, uncontrollable, side splitting laughter. It was as if Sheriff Andy Taylor thought he was doing something nice for his friends in Mayberry by baking them a Pecan pie and they all turned on him! He grabbed his photos and stomped off with the finger on both hands in the "flip-off" position, now that was funny. Stupid, but funny.

At one point the boat was under repairs in Dong Tam and I overhead a couple of guys talking about how somebody on the base was sending ham radio phone calls back to the states. They used a relay system to make a call to your city back home. I decide to walk over to the area where the calls were being made. Surprisingly there were only a couple of guys waiting in line to give it a shot. The guy running the show asked me where home was and I said Phoenix, Arizona. He said that I was in luck, Senator Barry Goldwater from Arizona was doing the call relays from his home in Phoenix. He asked me for my parents' home phone number. After 3 or 4 failed tries I suddenly heard Senator Goldwater on the headphones talking to my mom and giving her instructions on how this was going to work and my mom was simply crying into the phone. The senator told my mom that after every sentence she must say the words "over" before I could talk. She was crying so hard that finally Senator Goldwater says "over" for her and tells me to talk. It was so long ago now that I really do not remember what was said on that very short call, but at least my mom knew I was safe, and I felt really good about that.

Vietnam was a trip for me. I wasn't afraid to fight or mix it up with the gooks, but I was deadly afraid of dying as I knew I was going straight to hell. There was no question in my mind that I was a great combat fighter, still I believed I was a really horrible person who was not living up to the moral codes that my parents raised me with. My family would never in a million years understand my behavior of participating in every vice in the book. I often thought about how grateful I was that I was not married when I was in the Navy. I could rationalize and justify my smoking dope or having sex with the locals as a way to get through the weeks and months of fear and drudgery, yet always knowing in the back of my mind that my family would be devastated if they really knew what my life was like there. I had no clue that when I signed up for this duty that the place was such a hell hole. Also if it really sucked for me, what was life really like for the people who lived there and how did they feel about what was going on around them every day, for years at a stretch? It was mind boggling.

I got most of my news updates from the States from the constant flow of new faces I saw every week. Guys died or went home missing an arm or leg and they'd send in somebody to replace them. These were the people I would get my news from. I knew the war was not popular or supported back home, but I had no clue how much the boots on the ground were hated by the general population in the U.S. I didn't know that the soldiers in the field were personally being blamed for the Vietnam War.

A few weeks after I got home a friend from high school invited me to a party that he said would have a lot of girls I went to high school with, which got my attention. I was ready for a little fun, so that weekend he picked me up and we went to the party. I did see a lot of people I went to school with and suddenly a girl I knew came up to me and gave me a big hug and asked me where I had been hiding for the last four years. I told her I just got back from Vietnam and her face suddenly became unfriendly, she turned around and walked off. I was puzzled by her reaction until we were on our way home that night. My buddy told me that if I wanted to score with chicks and get dates that I should stop telling them that I just got back from Vietnam. He said tell them anything but that. It pissed me off, but that night was my very first clue on how much people hated the Vietnam War and the especially the guys who fought in it. That trend continued for me for the next 15 years. There were two letters that I did receive during my tour that were very sad for me and did nothing to boost my morale. One was from the mother of a guy I grew up with in Phoenix. She sent a newspaper clipping and a letter telling me that my friend's dad in Phoenix blew his head off in a suicide. My friend's father was a good guy who always went out of his way to be kind to me when I was a kid. I found it very strange that every day I woke up I was doing everything in my power to be safe, taking all the precautions I could take not to die in this war; when on the other hand this guy, who seemed to have everything, blew his head off in the safety of his personal $100,000 Jaguar. It made no sense to me.

The other letter I received was from my high school girl friend who informed me that her brother was killed in a car accident two weeks after arriving home from combat in Vietnam. He and his buddies got drunk and he killed himself in a car wreck. 'Shit' I think, what a horrible event this is! I felt bad for her and her family. I lie, I really did not feel bad for her, as she dumped me before I ever left for the Navy. This was the only letter she sent me my whole tour. I guess she felt I didn't have enough grief in my life as it was, so why not write a sad letter about her brother and make me feel even worse? I really did feel bad for her parents though. I guess my cold heart felt little sadness for her.

CHAPTER 14

THE FALL OF 1968

The summer of 1968 ended and the luck of our crew had held with no deaths or serious injuries. Operations continued and the rumor persisted that the MRF would either fold or be handed over to the ARVN sometime in the next few months. I had really tapered off of the opium, as I had seen the light at the end of the tunnel and I wanted to clear my head before going home in early 1969. I did not need to be a dope-head back in the world. I had purposely waited till the end of 1968 to request R&R as I wanted to go to Australia just before I was scheduled to go home. I had decided not to stay in the Navy and I just wanted to get back to my family in one piece. We continued to make enemy contact in the fall and every operation was still extremely dangerous. So I watched what I did daily, making no mistakes.

I put in for R&R for the month of December in late October. It turned out that Australia was a huge R&R destination and I wanted to make sure I got that as my first choice. Sometime in November I was told I had been approved for R&R in the middle of December for one week in Sydney. I was really jacked up for this vacation. I packed light for the week and took only what I needed in one carry-on, leaving the rest of my stuff on the boat.

We were paid in "scrip" or cash weekly by the military, I had plenty of scrip to convert to dollars when I got to Saigon. So money was not a problem. I could not wait to get to Australia. Finally around December 15, 1968 I caught a hop on a chopper into Saigon. I went through the process of R&R and boarded a plane full of Australian troops headed home. I prepared for the long flight ahead. After one stop for fuel in northern Australia we landed in Sydney. All of the Americans on the flight were bussed to a hotel in the King's Cross area of town. We were ushered into a big ballroom and were given our orientation on protocol for R&R behavior. Then we were assigned our hotels. We were also informed that there would be a big social dance that night in the hotel ballroom and that a lot of locals, like as in girls, would be there. I was bussed to my hotel, checked in and got to my room. Then I almost immediately left to find the closest bar, or in this case "pub," to get a tall, ice-cold beer.

I found a pub close to my hotel. When I walked into the place I noticed two things immediately . . . there was a small group of Aussie soldiers standing at the bar, and the bar had no seats, only standing room at the counter. I walked up to the bar and ordered a draft beer and the bartender draws the beer and sets it in front of me. I noticed it had no frothy head. Sadly, the beer was not ice-cold, just slightly chilled. The good news was that the alcohol content was a whopping 6% compared to the meager 3.2% back in the states! So I started my Australian vacation on a high note.

One of the Aussie soldiers looked around at me and easily pegged me as a Yank. He invited me to stand at the bar with his group. I quickly learned that I wasn't actually drinking beer but rather, ale. I was crushed the ale was not cold, still my new friends were very warm and friendly, so I started to drink with them. After two Aussie ales I was pretty buzzed and really wanted to sit down to drink.

A challenge was soon made among the Aussies to drink the ale from a one liter glass boot, while sitting upright in a chair and downing the ale in as few gulps as possible. Prior to Vietnam I would have considered myself a "healthy" beer drinker and able to keep up with anyone. Again that was with the 3.2% garden variety American beer. Attempting to impress my Aussie friends, I volunteered to go first with the glass boot and I began to slug down the ale. I learned later that as the ale pours out, an air bubble forms at the heel of the boot and the trick is to flick your wrist to pop the bubble, which then allowed the ale to flow smoothly and quickly. Because I was not aware of this flicking technique I was not the quickest drinker but I did win the prize for the first to get drunk. Quite simply that Aussie ale kicked my ass and I decided to stick to the 3.2% and drink it ice cold when available. After a cooling off period and with the assistance of two of the Aussie's, I was escorted back to the hotel. Hopefully I could sober up enough to attend the dance social only a few hours away.

Sydney was an outstandingly clean and friendly city. I knew I had made the right decision for my R&R choice. Vietnam was the farthest thing from my mind at the time. I was excited that I only had a few short weeks remaining after I returned to the boats. For the first time I thought I had a real chance of surviving the war.

The large ballroom was full of people and the social director had provided plenty of finger foods and soft drinks. Believe it or not there were a lot of young Australian girls there for our dancing pleasure. I had heard that some of these girls were looking for a free pass to the states by trying to hook up with, and marry, Americans on R&R. I could see that this would be an easy thing to do, like if one of these beautiful young girls came up to me, spoke in that great, sexy accent and asked "will you marry me?" at that point in my life I might just say yes.

I was not a dancer but sometime after I arrived, a very pretty, dark haired girl approached me and we danced a few times, but mostly we sat in the corner and talked. I had thought just before arriving in Sydney that any girl who got close to me would be in danger of finding a really horny guy, who might come across as being a little too aggressive. Yet as I sat and talked to her, sex was not my main focus, it *was* a focus, but not the main one. It was just nice to be able to talk to a girl who spoke English, who was my age and had some common interests.

Towards the end of the night I invited her back to my room, she accepted and we headed out for my hotel. As I sat and talked with this very pretty girl, I noticed that my anxiety level had dropped to almost zero. I was very comfortable with the conversation. I thought to myself that I was actually acting normal. Hopefully the abnormal state I had been living in for months was taking an R&R break as well. It gave me hope that I might be able to act normally around my family when I returned home. The girl was actually shy, but very polite, and the short of it was we slept in the same bed that night but did not have sex. We made out a little but no sex. I saw her two more times that week and even wrote to her after I returned home, but nothing really ever clicked. After time I lost contact with her.

It did, however, take no time for the man in me to kick in. I decided I did not have much time to wine and dine girls to get some sex. So, I decided to pay for a prostitute, a professional girl of my choice. Where better to get that information then from a local cab driver? Outside of my hotel was a cab stand and I jumped in the first one in line and told the driver what I was looking for. I had never been in a car where the driver was on the right hand side of the car and I was just as intrigued with the cars and the roads as I was in finding a "date." The cabbie tells me that prostitutes are decriminalized in the King's Cross area and finding what I wanted was an easy thing to do. He said he thought he knew what I was looking for, so he drove me to a nightclub several minutes away from the hotel. When we arrived he told me that any female I saw sitting at the tables in the back of the club were working girls, most of them would be about my age. It was around 8:00 PM and I wanted to do this quickly and get out of this club. I felt uneasy, as I saw no other American servicemen in the club. Still, I took the cabby at his word. I walked in and the club was actually a long narrow bar with low lights and some music coming from the rear and maybe fifty people total, sitting around the bar area. I walked to the back of the bar and I saw three younger girls sitting together at one table. The one in the middle caught my eye. I was a battle hardened veteran, yet my heart rate jumped with anticipation and I took the leap and sat down at the table. The girl in the middle stayed seated and the other 2 got up from the table and walked away. The cabbie was correct, they were all working girls, but now I was stuck not knowing what to do next. She asked me if I was a Yank and if I was in Sydney for R&R? I nodded my head yes. Then she asked me if I was looking for a "date," and I nodded my head yes again. She wanted to know my age and I told her. She told me I looked about 15 years old and scared. "Are you a virgin?" she asked, and I smiled and say, "No, mam." That broke the ice and I started to feel more at ease, we had a few ales. By now it was late and she told me the price for her services, which I agreed to.

We got into a cab and went back to my hotel. As we were walking through the lobby the front desk clerk yelled out at her and said something about no prostitutes allowed up the elevators to the rooms. She gave out a moan and turned around telling me to follow her. We jumped into another cab and she told me that we were going to her "flat" (apartment), but then she told me that she had to go back to work later that morning and I would have to leave as soon as we were done.

I know this sounds nuts, but something about her was sweet and innocent, she had a very cute smile and honestly I had not even checked out her body yet. I was just happy to be with a young girl my age. The paying up front for love did not bother me. We arrived at her flat, went up a flight of stairs and entered what I would call a one bedroom apartment, very neat and organized. The room even had a nice view of the city. She brought out a couple of cold beers (finally an ice cold *beer*, not slightly cool ale!) and told me that she was going to take a shower and for me to make myself at home. This sure beat the crap out of the rivers in Nam. For the first time since arriving in Sydney I was totally relaxed and enjoying myself. She returned from her shower and asked

112

if I would like to shower as well. I thought it was a good idea to go into the bathroom, take 10 minutes or so and return to the bedroom.

When I came in she was sitting on the bed with a cover-up type dress on and she was very cute, smiling and asking me how I liked Sydney. I was enjoying myself so much that sex was not on my mind, so we sat on the bed for 30 minutes or so, just drinking beer and talking. This is not how I envisioned it would be with a professional prostitute, but I was glad she was friendly and she looked in my eyes when we talked. I never even got this kind of conversation from any of the girls I went to high school with, this was fantastic!

It was now 1:00 AM and it was show time. She pulled off her cover-up and asked me to please sit on the edge of the bed naked with her. I complied and she reached over and grabbed my penis and moved it around like someone milking the tit of a cow. "I'm honestly not trying to get you excited," she said. "I'm looking for any signs of Hanoi Jack." She explained to me that Hanoi Jack was a deadly venereal disease brought to South Vietnam by North Vietnamese soldiers and passed on to the Americans by South Vietnamese women. It produced a white puss and was highly dangerous. She wanted to make sure I was clean.
Sadly, at that point I thought of Doug Morton, who had told me back in California that he has contracted the "Black VD" while in the Philippines. This was, at the time, an incurable form of VD with no known antibiotic to fix the problem. He had expressed his concern over the VD and he had hoped that before he got out of the military there would be some way that the VD could be eliminated. For him, that was not to be. I passed the VD test and by 2:00 AM I was very tired and she was ready to go back to work. After I paid her she told me that I was very sweet and that I may stay and sleep in her bed until 6:30 AM, but I needed to be out by 7:00 AM. I was surprised that she trusted me. I fell to sleep and was awakened by an alarm set at precisely 6:30 AM. Believe it or not that was the best night of my military life. I took a quick shower and headed back to the hotel.

The rest of my R&R was predictably routine, plenty of drinking in the pubs, not much sightseeing and then it was time to go back to Saigon and resume my tour.

CHAPTER 15

THE END IS NEAR

I flew back to Saigon and bunked down at the R&R center and waited for a hop back to Dong Tam. I had very mixed emotions about returning to the boats. The short time I spent in Sydney recharged my batteries for life, the atmosphere in Australia was like back home in the states. The thought of going back to the boats for a couple of operations actually sickened my stomach. I was so close to the finish line that going back to the boats to run one or two more operations seemed like one big fucking stupid chance to take, but what choice did I have? I was actually very nervous and I really hoped that somehow I would be prevented from returning to the C-112-1.

At that point I was flat broke after spending nearly all my money in Australia. I still had a few days to kill before finding a hop back to the boats. I spent a couple of nights in the bar district of Saigon and by the looks of the place you would never know there was a war going on around us. The streets were filled with bars, whores and American music. Every bar I went into was a party with GI's from every service. I spent my last few dollars drinking and worrying a lot about going home. I was not the same guy I was when I arrived in Nam and I was afraid my family would freak out when they saw the person I had become. Sad to say but I was a lost soul at that point. I remembered being actually too drunk to walk and begging from strangers for a little change to get another drink on the streets of Saigon.

Finally after a few days I got a hop out of that party town and arrived back to Dong Tam. It was December 23rd and I went to the base bar to grab a beer. I nodded hello to a guy about my age sitting next to me and we started to talk. I told him I was only a few weeks away from going home and I really hated the fact that I had to return to the boat; it was like tempting fate this close to going home. He told me that the Bob Hope show was going to be held Christmas day at the base and if I was still there maybe I would like to go. I told him hell yes I'd like to go! And it appeared that this guy had the inside ticket to get me a good seat. I sat around all day on the 24th waiting for a hop to the boat. For some reason it was not to be that day. So I headed back to the bar on Christmas Eve and my new friend was there. He told me that he had a

114

seat for the show and that I was more than welcome to join him and his buddies. He told me that he worked in Navy Personnel and that he wanted to be on the river boats too, but he got stuck in this office job. He said, "it was not supposed to be" and that he wasn't complaining. He told me the meeting place to be in the morning. I was really excited to see the Bob Hope show, especially on Christmas day.

I don't remember what time the show started, but it was a packed house and sometime during the show some VC across the river caught the attention of some Huey gunships and they opened fire while Bob Hope was on stage. He made some crude joke about the VC and went on with the show like nothing happened.

Growing up our family watched the Bob Hope Christmas Special yearly. To have this experience as a part of my Vietnam tour was very exciting. What I did not realize as a kid was how "blue" the jokes actually were and how much editing must have been done to air that show on American TV. Bob Hope used the F word as often as a drunken sailor. Still, it was some fucking funny stuff he spat out, constant rapid fire one-liners, one after the other. He ragged on the Army generals and the Navy admirals, he used sexist jokes and nasty body language when the Dean Martin Gold Digger dancers came out on stage. He made light of the "pussies" who were protesting the war back in the world. The last two weeks had been very good to me, a great vacation in Australia and the Bob Hope Show live gave me the opportunity to relax and laugh myself to tears in-country, something that had not happened in the last eleven and a half months. When the show was over, my new friend told me what building he worked in and asked me to stop by before I caught my ride to the boat, I thanked him for inviting me to the show and I went to bed.

I was flat broke after spending every dime I had in Australia and I was thinking about getting a draw against my pay before getting a hop out on the 26th of December. I found my way to the building that this guy worked in, and as he sees me walk through the door, he grabs a large manila envelope off his desk and he walks towards me. Now I knew what was in that envelope, because it is what all servicemen carry when they travel from one duty station to another. On the outside are the travel orders taped to the envelope. Inside is your service jacket. I did not know why he was carrying this to me. He approached me, handed me the envelope and says, "Merry Christmas, you're going home." I was a tough guy, but my knees began to buckle with excitement and I asked him to explain. He told me that he had the connections to end my tour in Vietnam, that my service record and pay were inside the envelope, and all I had to do was catch a hop to Saigon and muster out of the country, which might take a few days. I was in shock! I blurted out that all I had to wear was my green fatigues, that all of my other uniforms were on my boat. He pointed out that on the travel orders were the words: "Authorized to wear fatigues to CONUS (Continental United States).

This guy had thought of *everything* and I did not know what to say. I was actually going home and I was too excited to think! He shook my hand and walked back to his desk and I felt like a little kid on Christmas morning.

As excited as I was, I still had that creepy sensation return to me about going home to my family. Then a new thought popped into my head. I wouldn't be able to collect my personal belongings on the boat. Plus I started to think that perhaps I might be turning my back on my crew, my Brown Water Navy family who I'd spent a very long and difficult eleven and a half months with. I returned to my bunk area and began to ponder if this sudden event was good fortune for me or if I was running out on my crew, I had a very tough time sleeping that night. The next morning I gathered my stuff and hiked over to the staging area, clutching my manila envelope tightly, and signed the sheet for a hop to Saigon. My name was called and I was assigned to a helicopter for the trip to Saigon. I still had not decided if this sudden trip home was a good thing or not. I decided that fate had intervened, so I calmed myself and waited for the Huey to take off.

When I arrived in Vietnam my biggest fear was dying and going to hell, I cannot stress this enough. However, as the months passed by and my R & R to Australia approached, I had this giddy feeling inside that I might have a legitimate shot of making it out of this hell hole and reuniting with my family in one piece. My soul, sadly, did not share my physical body's reaction to this good news, as I was afraid of returning home a completely different human being than my family remembered. I had a fractured soul when I left Vietnam on January 1, 1969, and I did not have a plan A or B to fix it. I knew I was different than I had been before I arrived for my twelve month tour. I was not especially happy with the end results, or even grateful to God for allowing me to come home alive. I thought I would be over the moon with excitement on the flight home but the moon's dark side hovered over my head and I was desperately thinking about how I would act around my family in a normal, Charlie-like way.

I caught a hop on a Huey helicopter to Tan Son Nhut Air Base in Saigon, and waited to be mustered out of country, which should only have taken a few days. I sat at the same airfield that I had arrived at about one year ago, full circle from start to finish.

For two days I chained smoked. I kept to myself. I had no desire to strike up conversations with strangers and swap war stories. Many thoughts ran through my head while waiting for that flight out. I watched hundreds of men coming and going. I simply had no energy left to worry about seeing my family in a few short days. I told myself simply to watch my language, not to smoke in front of my family, certainly do not tell war stories to my mother and finally to push Doug Morton out of my head for good. I felt at the time that Doug Morton was a part of the past and I wanted to move on. I thought that I would visit his mother after I returned home and be done with it. That would close the book on Vietnam for me. Au contraire, foolish me, not in a million years.

After a very long flight we touched down at night in Oakland. There we had to sit on the tarmac for nearly two hours waiting for customs to complete their inspection of the plane. After unloading, I went to this area where I was told that tomorrow morning I would catch a bus to the Naval Facility at Treasure Island in San Francisco. There I was to process out of the navy and that took approximately seven days to complete. I was told I could sleep on the floor in the terminal, or walk to one of the airport hotels that were close to the terminal. I chose to go to a hotel for the night. I wanted a hot shower, a clean bed and a very cold American beer. Since I only had the fatigues that I was wearing and no luggage it was an easy walk. I was just looking around at everything like I had never been to America before. Beautiful American girls were everywhere. I was so thankful to be so close to home.

I went to the front desk and got a room. I asked the clerk if there was a place to eat near the hotel. He suggested that I take room service. He wanted to know if I just arrived from overseas and I told him yes, Vietnam. He said something to effect of welcome back. I did not think much about his comment and I went up to my room. My fatigues were dirty and I smelled to high heaven so I took a shower and ordered a ham sandwich and an ice cold beer from room service. When the food arrived I asked the service guy if it would be possible to get my fatigues laundered overnight, to which he replied yes. So I put them in a plastic bag and the room service guy took them to be cleaned. He told me that my clothes would be hanging on the outside of the door by 7:00 AM tomorrow morning. Before he left the room I wanted to settle up on the food and the laundry bill. He catches me totally off guard. He tells me, "No charge, compliments of the hotel night manager." I asked if he was serious. He said yes, said goodnight and left the room. Wow. That was unexpected.

For the first time since arriving back in the states I was alone with my thoughts. The idea of closing the book on Vietnam did not last more than a day. I lay on the hotel bed with my eyes wide open, unable to sleep. I started to reflect on the past year and how the Vietnam War was really fought in the areas I operated in. I had decided after four months into my tour that the war was a lost cause, that the American strategy of search and destroy was pure bullshit. If you killed 30 VC in a firefight they would replace them with 60 guys the next day, when Doug Morton was killed it probably took two to three weeks to replace him. You could drop bombs and kill these people all day long and it didn't matter to them, they were not afraid to die, I was, we all were, but not the enemy. I reflected on how gung-ho I was when I first arrived, yet as the operations and months passed, I had become more convinced that the MRF was in a losing fight, and that on some operations the boats were just sitting ducks waiting to be picked off.

I knew in my heart that many more souls would die for many years to come, and I was very grateful that I made it back states. I also thought that I had made the proper decision not to extend my tour in Vietnam and hoped that the MRF would be dissolved in the near future to save more sailor's lives. I did believe that the MRF kicked some serious ass, but wondered if it was worth the price.
Now that I got those thoughts out of my head I could finally close the book on Vietnam, lol.

Why this recent good luck had happened to me. I did not know, but I was grateful and I consumed the beer and ham sandwich and fell asleep. I got up early, and as promised, my fatigues were hanging on the door freshly starched and pressed. I walked back over to the terminal and minutes later was on a bus heading for Treasure Island, the drive was great and I took in every sight and smell I could, I missed my country and was so glad to be home.

I checked in at the desk and was assigned a bunk. I was told it would take 5 or 6 days to muster out of the Navy. The rules were very simple, while waiting for my discharge there would be no liberty or leaving the base. I had the choice to work a detail or sit around and do nothing for the next 5 or 6 days. Me? I chose to do nothing. I slept a lot, watched a very small screen black & white TV, smoked cigarettes and stayed to myself, I was not in the mood to be sociable and tell war stories, all I wanted was peace and quiet.

On day five I was called in to take a physical in the medical clinic along with seven or eight other guys. I stripped naked and stood facing the doctor waiting for him to exam the exterior of our bodies. I was a bit nervous at this point because a few days earlier I had noticed a large bump on the bottom side of my penis while taking a shower. The bump was hard and almost red in color. It actually ran through my mind that I had contracted the "Hanoi Jack" which would be a real problem for me. The Navy wasn't going to cut me loose with a case of VD. The doctor stood in front of me. He was wearing rubber gloves. He lifted up my genitals and took a look. I knew he must have seen the bump. He told me to turn around, face the wall, bend over and spread 'em, which I did. After a second he says, "Okay turn around," and before he moves on to the guy next to me tells me I should pop that pimple on my penis. Now that is what I call relief!

On day six I was called into an office and was told to go to a room and take a seat. In the room was a Navy guy with my service jacket on his desk. He was very direct and unfriendly. He told me that if I wanted to "ship over" and extend my Navy service this is what the Navy is offering: 15 days leave, my choice of one of three duty stations, $1000 cash bonus and a chance for a promotion within the first 30 days of my extension. I asked if I had to take a written test for the promotion and he replied "yes."

Now this moment was a pivotal point in my life, I was on the cusp of making the Navy a career or turning away and going down the civilian road. I had given this moment a lot of thought and after a minute or two I told the guy I wasn't not interested and signed-off for my separation from the Navy. "Okay," he says and tells me that sometime the next day they will have my papers in order, along with a plane ticket to Phoenix, and I would be free to go. As I walked towards the door the guy says, "Don't do anything stupid for the next 72 hours, your ass still belongs to the United States Navy." I saluted him and walked out the door.

The sad part about the process I had just completed was that at no time during my stay waiting to be separated was I approached and asked if I had any questions or concerns. No shrink checked me out to see if I was raving lunatic coming straight over from combat. Nobody asked if I had anxiety attacks or bad dreams, or if I had any thoughts about killing myself. Even if someone had asked me questions I didn't like, it would have shown me that my military was concerned about my wellbeing prior to be released back into civilian life. Even a "Fuck you, get out of here," would have been nice. A diagnosis of Post-traumatic stress disorder for Vietnam combat veterans was still a twinkle in some psychiatrist's eye when I was discharged in 1969. I honestly think that the military could have cared less if I had nightmares or not. I didn't think I needed any help then, so why would the military think I needed any help either?

On January 1, 1969 I blasted off the dark surface of the moon and headed back to my world. I arrived back in Phoenix on January 9th, 1969 to the loving arms of my family and to a Christmas party my family had for me! The entire family waited till I got home to have their Christmas along with me on January 9th. That was pretty special.

I think looking back I did my best to hide my emotions from family but the truth is I was in emotional pain for many years. I now perceived myself as the black sheep of the family who was unable to fit in. When I got back to the world I began to jump from job to job and move from city to city. I couldn't settle down. I couldn't stay calm. I loved my family but my experience in Vietnam triggered some type of resistance to a normal stable life in one spot, I had the urge to move around and search for a purpose and a meaning for my life.

For decades afterwards I had mixed emotions about the sudden departure from Vietnam. I often wondered what my crew thought about me after I did not return from R & R. I never saw or talked to any of my crew again after my departure from Vietnam. I felt and still feel I should have made an effort, but like the death of my friend Doug, I wanted to leave it all behind and build a new life for myself, sadly for me it didn't work out that way.

The first fifteen years after my separation from the Navy were unpleasant and hard for me mentally, it was not uncommon for me to have a bad attitude, waking up from a dead sleep gasping for air and going through numerous jobs I could not hold down for no apparent reason.

I never followed the war after I got home, if I saw a news report on TV I simply flicked the channel to get away from it. I think the strategy of America to "win" never changed for the duration of the war and it would sadden me anytime I heard bad news coming from there. I'm proud as punch of my service and even prouder of the MRF efforts for the few years they were in operation but I'm glad the MRF pulled out when they did, in the long run it saved many Brown Water sailors lives.

To the casual observer who reads about my account in Vietnam, they may think that year was a success for me. Yes, I did survive the war when so many did not, but I guess it is how you define the word success. The efforts of the MRF sailors went largely unnoticed even though their daily sacrifices were at stratospheric levels. I believe the MRF overall was a logistical failure led by flawed commanders. I think that the American effort at all levels was one big cluster fuck from beginning to end, with no sensible strategy to win or even end the war. Our enemies were nearly invisible. 50 yards into the tree line and we were on their home turf for God's sake! The enemy was dug in through the entire country with a network of tunnels, supply lines and spies that was nearly impenetrable. We turned friendlies into hostiles because you could not burn their villages to the ground and fill their rice paddies with bomb craters and expect them to adore you.

During my entire tour I never gave a rat's ass about the Viet Cong, our enemy. My only concern was my self-preservation and the safety of the boat and crew. It was not until years later after fighting my own Vietnam demons that I wondered about the Viet Cong, the ones who survived years of fighting. If twelve months in Vietnam flipped me over as a person, what could years on the battlefield do to the mind and soul of these soldiers? Their tours of duty were measured in years, not months. The big difference of course was they had a reason to fight what they thought was an invasion of their country. Also, they were not afraid to die, in some cases they could not wait to die, to enter Paradise. I'm no expert but I would assume the average VC had no R & R privileges, were not given a government funeral after dying in battle, nor had any special health care provided for them after the war. I wondered if PTSD was a condition only known to the Western World or if they too had bad dreams year after year? I've had no animosity towards the Vietnamese people in the last 46 years and I'm curious if a VC combat veteran in my age group would still despise the Americans for invading his country?

I think the main difference between our two cultures was their willingness to be patient to achieve their goals in comparison to our culture of "go big or go home." The NVA generals knew that time was on their side and the American public would grow weary of the Vietnam War. Sadly those same generals were willing to sacrifice the lives of over one million of their own people to achieve their goals and that does not include the lives lost fighting the French.

My decision to volunteer for combat was not politically motivated in any way, it was simply my desire to experience combat first hand. I did not have a choice of what war to participate in, Vietnam was the only war on the table at the time. There were never any conversations between the crew if the war was right or wrong, should we stay or should we go. It was what it was and we accepted the cards that were dealt to us every day.

What I took away from my training early on was this, we are Americans and we will go anywhere in the world and kill the bad guys. We, as Americans, are the heroes and we will try to make a difference in the world which makes our lives and others, honorable and worthy. The VC, NVA, generals and dictators, and all the people like them who take life to be meaningless, and those who want everyone to march in lockstep for the "State," deserve to die and we will wipe them away forever, their lives mean nothing compared to ours, because we are the Americans. This became clear to me during my tour as I could witness 10 or 15 dead VC who all died a horrible death and that sight would not affect me in any manner. But if I saw one dead American, brown white or black, I would get a chill down my back and I felt very sad. After all the VC deserved to die, but we did not, not a pleasant way to think for a 20 year old man.

I know that the sailors who served with the MRF where tough sons of bitches, many may have questioned some of the Command's decisions but they continued on with the mission with little complaining. The MRF is unknown to most people who have read Vietnam War stories and even to some who consider themselves knowledgeable about Vietnam combat units. Every sailor on those boats put out as much or more effort as any other combat unit in Vietnam. I was never guilt-ridden about my role in the war, I was then and still now proud of my service with the MRF and especially to Douglas George Morton and all KIA sailors of the MRF.

On the American front, I never disliked or held a grudge against anti-war protestors back home, I thought they had every right to protest in the streets, if this is what they were compassionate about that was okay with me. What I did not like however were high profile celebrities who used their fame as a platform to protest the war, many who blamed the boots on the ground soldiers for the war. It was the draft dodgers who fled the country to avoid serving that I did not like. To me those types were civilian deserters who were selfish and should not have been allowed to return home to the states. Still, in the 46 years since leaving Vietnam I have never told as much as one war story to any member of my family, let alone a stranger. I have kept my comments about Vietnam to myself, thinking quite honestly nobody would care to listen to them, the war was so hated by everybody I thought that the best policy was silence.

When I think about my year in-country it is usually about the daily hardships and struggles of being away from my family, and about my close bond to my crew on C-112-1. I rarely thought about the combat side of the story. My story is unusual I think because I knew somebody I served with prior to joining the Navy and it is really a pleasure to think about him and not a sorrowful memory like some might think.

The bottom line for me in this entire experience was that I believed I was a living, breathing coward who could not face the one thing I really wanted and needed to do in this life, that was to go visit Doug Morton's mother who only lived a few short miles from my parents' home. Every Memorial Day forward from 1969 was an agonizing torturous day for me as I would promise myself to go visit Mrs. Morton. But I could never gather the courage to do it. I thought that she might hate me for surviving while Doug died and I did not want to face that possibility.

Maybe if I would have manned up and not acted like a coward I could have said something to make a difference with her. I had now become the same coward who fled the country to avoid the draft, the same guy who I felt should not be allowed back into the country. This is something that I will never be able to forget for the rest of my life. I had the courage to volunteer for combat in Vietnam but not the balls to face a middle-aged woman, when maybe that would have been just what she needed to help her heal. Vietnam supplied me with more than bad memories and the loss of life of a friend from Phoenix. It robbed me of learning the tradition of treating my superiors with respect. There was a general loss of common sense, a lack of respect or empathy for others who were disadvantaged, and my great loss of faith in God and the hope for a brighter future. With some hard work all of these losses were regained as my time away from Vietnam grew and I eventually became the same ol' lovable guy I was before my tour. Vietnam was a "head game" for me. It was a "head space" where I might as well had been on the dark side of the moon for those 12 months. Because for me it was not like the planet earth that I thought I knew.

It wasn't until the last five or six years that I learned that these events and feelings I had been having all these years are common symptoms of PTSD, post-traumatic stress disorder. I used to think I was having a heart attack and I would wonder why I had no chest pains. I thought when you had a heart attack it was painful. I simply did not understand what I was going through at the time. In the end I think after forty plus years I have beaten the PTSD.

Strangely, after having recorded all these experiences, I would not change a thing about my time in Vietnam. If I had to do it all over again, I would do it. I'm glad I volunteered my service. I often pray that my friend Doug Morton and all of the fallen of Vietnam did not die in vain. In my tour of Vietnam many Brown Water sailors lost arms or legs. Doug Morton lost his life. I'm positive every single one of us suffered and lost something just as important, that is, our God given right to a safe and happy teenage life, untouched by violence and hate.

Truthfully I would love to go visit Vietnam today and travel back to the small canals and waterways of my youth. I would occasionally watch the sunset after a very long, stressful day and think to myself that if you could cut through all of the bullshit that was Vietnam, it probably would be an okay country to live in. When you are 20 years old, working and living in a war zone, you are not exactly a romantic, you become cynical and depressed quickly but there were moments when I viewed the world around me with eyes wide open, wondering if the effort made by the Americans was helping or hurting the people of South Vietnam. To this day I really do not know the answer to that thought.

Finally on Memorial Day 2012, I was able to locate where Doug had been laid to rest in Phoenix, and I finally went out to his gravesite and I was able to make peace with myself and Doug's family. I am now trying to find out if my friend had a military burial and if he has any living relatives.

I now visit Doug as often as I can and my wife always makes him a very nice new flower arrangement that we proudly put at his grave. The discovery of Doug's grave has finally closed this chapter in my life, a chapter I now never want to forget. So the transition back to the World is now complete and the transformation back to myself has begun. I'm not the same person I was when I arrived in Vietnam. However, I can say that my experience in Vietnam influenced me all of my life, which, in the end, I think is a good thing.

AFTERWARD

ABOUT THE EDITOR

At first I was just going to put this book on my computer and not tell anyone about it. I was just going to let someone find it after I died. I didn't feel good about telling my kids, grandkids, and my family about what I had done in the war. I had some guilt about the drugs, the VD and the violence. I had not done well after my service either. I really just wanted to write a memoir and let others deal with it later. I thought that would clear my mind. Then I began to think about Doug Morton. How we had been friends, how he had died and I had survived. I thought about all those like Doug forgotten in that war. I wanted the story told. I wanted to show what we all went through. What I went through. So I changed my mind. I realized if I was going to publish and promote this book, then I needed some professional assistance. That's where David St. Albans comes in. I found him at http://saintalbansstudio here in Scottsdale Az. He seemed like he had the skills I needed. So I contacted him. What I hadn't realized was that he was an antiwar protester in Chicago and L.A. during the time I was in Vietnam. As I fought to keep South Vietnam and America free, he was fighting to bring soldiers like me home and end the war. How did two completely different political/religious/cultural guys wind up collaborating on a book about Nam? Well, I believe God brought us together to make this happen. Because it was a bad and tragic war for everyone, in-country and back in the World. David respected the commitment guys like me had made. He understood that Doug Morton did not get his chance, because he was fighting an unwinable and protracted war that kept a lot of young Americans from living their part of the American Dream. But here, let Dave tell you his story . . .

Hello, my name is David Pudelwitts-St. Albans. I am a professional artist, editor and writer. I have been running my own editing and graphics company now for going on five years. I have edited about ten books so far. Before that I did fine art, illustration, editorial writing and publishing in my spare time for over 35 years. I've run two art galleries in the Southwest, had my own Wild West Show and Tour and my own publishing company. Everything I did on my own was creative or helping

126

other creative people with their work. Like Charlie though, I've had a lot of regular jobs in sales and retail over the years.

Recently I got a call from Charlie Nesbitt and was intrigued that he wanted to write his memoir of the time he served in Vietnam. I had to tell him up front that I was an Anti-War Protester back in the day. And when I say that, I mean that I was *at* the Democratic National Convention in Chicago when I was 12. I marched in dozens of protest marches in Chicago and Los Angeles from age 13 to 18. The war, to me, seemed endless, outrageous and illegal. I started when I was twelve and knew that when I was 18 I'd be shipped over there to die.

I joined the ROTC for a short time in my first year of high school in Chicago, Illinois, thinking if I had to go to war, I would at least go as an officer. But after the Democratic Convention and the riots that summer I marched in front of Mayor Daley of Chicago and flipped him the Bird. (You should have seen his face!) After that I became a radical. I even voted Socialist when they allowed us to vote at 18 in California. I did that just because I WANTED to be on the FBI list. I'd had it with my government. I protested the war for as long as it went on. I was chased by cops, had bottles thrown at my head, and chanted "Hell No We Won't Go!" I wanted to bring our troops home. The worst part of it was I saw so many people, including friends, come back from it so screwed up in the head with drugs, PTSD, nightmares, anxiety, and just plain feelings of confusion that I felt there was something horrible about it no one was talking about. I heard stories that curled my hair for sure. Then there was the Mai Lai massacre and other reports coming in that made it seem less like a war and more like a drug crazed free-for-all. We found out a lot of the heroin and opium coming into the U.S. was direct from the Cambodia/Thailand/Vietnam pipeline. Some of it being shipped in the caskets of our dead soldiers! I did not support the VC or the NVA and had no love for dictators like Mao or Ho Chi Minh. I did feel though that Richard Nixon, Bob McNamara, Zumwalt and others like them were no better morally or ethically than any other power mongers. I was a staunch advocate of bringing all the troops back home and ending a ten year long debacle.

In the end we lost the war altogether, and we saw the horrible effects it had on our politics, our economy, on our soldiers and on the whole country. It became the war no one wanted to speak about. The troops became invisible victims, rather than heroes. They were called names, spit on and eventually made fun of for their nightmares and their medical needs. However, I was not the sort of person that blamed our troops, I blamed our leaders.

At first, just like Doug and Charlie I wanted to fight. I thought the WWII vets and the Korean vets were heroes. I loved war movies and TV shows like "Combat!" I had played war as a kid. I like guns. I wanted to be a soldier. My father and uncle had been in the Navy during the Korean conflict. Others in my family had proudly done their duty since at least WWI. So I joined the ROTC in 1968, but when I saw how they trained us, to hate "gooks" and kill any "slopes" or "slants" that they demanded we kill, even 10 to 12 year old kids, I balked. After all I was only 13 myself.

After my stint in the ROTC I turned my back on a war machine that was using us, and them, as cannon fodder, and calling people "enemies" who had not invaded us or threatened the world in any meaningful way. I hated the men who were sending us to die. Yet I deeply respected the men who fought in that war. I told Charlie Nesbitt this. He considered my position and then determined to go ahead and use my talents to get his book out.

Charlie's book is an eye-opener. In his eleven and a half month stint as an MRF sailor he saw and experienced almost everything I had heard from other young men coming back in the 70's from the war. Those events and experiences almost seem to us these days, as the stuff of fantasy, the stuff of movies like Apocalypse Now and Platoon. But it was really the John Wayne movies of the 60's that were the fantasies that the War Department and the government wanted us to think was a reality. We were told that good men were dying for a just cause against a rabid "Communist" enemy who "hated our freedoms." This was never the case. It was more to me like throwing American boys into a meat grinder from which there was no escape, even after they got out. We were trying to stop the North from taking over the South. It was a civil war. In the end the North took over and instead of some horrible "Domino Effect," where the entire Asian subcontinent became Communist and a threat to American Security, we wound up with Vietnam as a resort vacation destination! We wasted souls, technology, money and machinery in a lost cause. We were wrong. The war was wrong. I just watched a program called "Nixon by Nixon: In His Own Words" turns out the war was extended for years just for political and power gains by men who could have cared less about American boys being slaughtered. You can hear it in Nixon's voice when he became enraged when our Air Force told him they wouldn't risk losing aircraft on a bombing run Nixon wanted done during a storm. Definitely the "Abnormal becoming Normal" in those bad old days.

The meat grinder Charlie went through was the real deal. My memories of the times and events of the Vietnam War were verified to be distinct and accurate, thanks to Charlie's flood of memories as he wrote his book. I wanted to find out more about his side of things, so I said I'd help him with his story. I also wanted the men who fought in that conflict who have become lost to history and who were truly fallen heroes, like Doug Morton, to be reintroduced to us, to be reinstated in a sense, to be brought back home and laid to rest with honor and dignity. Charlie's war is over. But the insanity of the war machine rolls on. What I fought against in 1969, still needs to be fought against today. I am still fighting.

What is really odd is that Charlie's attitude of basically telling authorities to F-off is exactly the same mentality I had state side. I liked my long hair too. I wore my vest with no shirt underneath as well. Of course I wore a lot of peace sign buttons and legalize hemp pins on my vest. I often wore military second-hand clothes. Once a veteran who picked me up hitchhiking offered me some really nice jungle boots. But my friend said "Don't wear them! You'll get the Jungle Rot and your feet will fall off! They're full of fungus!"

Like Charlie, I did tell a lot of authority figures to F-off starting with Chicago's Mayor Richard Daley. I smoked grass but never opium. I took a lot of acid and I drank heavily my last year in high school. I was pretty worried about the draft. When my number came up I was told I wouldn't be drafted anyway because I'd had an ulcer when I was 14. The army said: "Our food would kill you long before the gooks did!"

The days of the Vietnam War were heady times, full of a lot of political conflict. Yet none of that has come between Charlie and I. Charlie's a good guy. I seriously don't think he's going to hell, because he's been through the Valley of Death already. I think his book is his way of asking forgiveness. I sincerely hope people will read this story and start to ask questions. Charlie for instance, would love to find out if Doug Morton got a military funeral, and if not, would like to get him one now. Perhaps some of Charlie's old MRF mates will come forward and tell their stories. I think this is a worthy story and one which needed to be told. I am proud to help Doug, Charlie and all the vets of that war as best I can. I agree with Charlie in this, people of completely different views and beliefs can work together to make something happen. Which is exactly what America is all about.

David St. Albans, Scottsdale, AZ
2014

CONTACT PAGE

To contact the author, email Charlie Nesbitt at:
brownwaternavy@outlook.com

Check out his Facebook page at:
www.facebook.com/riverboatcombat here you will find photographs and 16 short videos taken by Charlie Nesbitt in 1968 when he was in-country. A valuable documentation of the times.

To contact the editor, email David St. Albans at:
whisperindave@msn.com

Check out his Facebook page at:
http://www.facebook.com/SaintAlbans1

Other sites you might be interested in:

Mobile Riverine Force at: http://www.mrfa.org/

Brown Water Navy website at: http://brownwater-navy.com/

16208809R00080

Made in the USA
San Bernardino, CA
23 October 2014